AF681166

The Art of Integrating Strategic Planning, Process Metrics, Risk Mitigation, and Auditing

Also available from ASQ Quality Press

Auditing Beyond Compliance: Using the Portable Universal Quality Lean Audit Model
Janet Bautista Smith

How to Establish a Document Control System for Compliance with ISO 9001:2015, ISO 13485:2016, and FDA Requirements: A Comprehensive Guide to Designing a Process-Based Document Control System
Stephanie L. Skipper

ISO 9001:2015 Explained, Fourth Edition
Charles A. Cianfrani, John E. "Jack" West, and Joseph Tsiakals

ISO 9001:2015 Internal Audits Made Easy, Fourth Edition
Ann W. Phillips

ISO 9001:2015 for Small and Medium-Sized Businesses, Third Edition
Denise Robitaille

The FDA and Worldwide Quality System Requirements Guidebook for Medical Devices, Second Edition
Amiram Daniel and Ed Kimmelman

Implementing ISO/IEC 17025:2005
Bhavan "Bob" Mehta

The Biomedical Quality Auditor Handbook, Second Edition
Biomedical Division and Bruce Haggar, editor

The Quality Toolbox, Second Edition
Nancy R. Tague

Root Cause Analysis: Simplified Tools and Techniques, Second Edition
Bjørn Andersen and Tom Fagerhaug

The Certified Six Sigma Green Belt Handbook, Second Edition
Roderick A. Munro, Govindarajan Ramu, and Daniel J. Zrymiak

The Certified Manager of Quality/Organizational Excellence Handbook, Fourth Edition
Russell T. Westcott, editor

The ASQ Auditing Handbook, Fourth Edition
J.P. Russell, editor

To request a complimentary catalog of ASQ Quality Press publications, call 800-248-1946, or visit our Web site at http://www.asq.org/quality-press.

The Art of Integrating Strategic Planning, Process Metrics, Risk Mitigation, and Auditing

J. B. Smith

ASQ Quality Press
Milwaukee, Wisconsin

American Society for Quality, Quality Press, Milwaukee, WI 53203
© 2016 by ASQ.
All rights reserved. Published 2015.
Printed in the United States of America.

21 20 19 18 17 16 5 4 3 2 1

Library of Congress Cataloging-in-Publication Data

Names: Smith, Janet B., 1954- author.
Title: Integration of strategic planning, performance metrics, and auditing / Janet B. Smith.
Description: Milwaukee, WI : ASQ Quality Press, 2016. | Includes index.
Identifiers: LCCN 2015049945 | ISBN 9780873899253 (hardcover; cd : alk. paper)
Subjects: LCSH: Strategic planning. | Performance—Measurement. | Auditing, Internal. | Management.
Classification: LCC HD30.28 .S5695 2016 | DDC 658.4/012—dc23
LC record available at http://lccn.loc.gov/2015049945

No part of this book may be reproduced in any form or by any means, electronic, mechanical, photocopying, recording, or otherwise, without the prior written permission of the publisher.

Publisher: Seiche Sanders
Acquisitions Editor: Matt T. Meinholz
Managing Editor: Paul Daniel O'Mara
Production Administrator: Randall Benson

ASQ Mission: The American Society for Quality advances individual, organizational, and community excellence worldwide through learning, quality improvement, and knowledge exchange.

Attention Bookstores, Wholesalers, Schools, and Corporations: ASQ Quality Press books, video, audio, and software are available at quantity discounts with bulk purchases for business, educational, or instructional use. For information, please contact ASQ Quality Press at 800-248-1946, or write to ASQ Quality Press, P.O. Box 3005, Milwaukee, WI 53201-3005.

To place orders or to request ASQ membership information, call 800-248-1946. Visit our Web site at www.asq.org/quality-press.

Printed on acid-free paper

ASQ
Quality Press
600 N. Plankinton Ave.
Milwaukee, WI 53203-2914
E-mail: authors@asq.org
The Global Voice of Quality™

Dedication

This book is dedicated to

Daniel and Scott.

Contents

The Art of War was the inspiration to this book's table of contents format. The *Art of War* is an ancient Chinese military treatise attributed to Sun Tzu, a high-ranking military general, strategist, and tactician. *The Art of War* has been applied to many fields well outside of the military. Much of the text is about how to fight wars without actually having to do battle. As such, it has found application as a training guide for many competitive endeavors that do not involve actual combat.

The Art of War chapter titles reflect an effective roadmap applicable to modern business strategic planning and management. The listing below shows the *The Art of War* chapter list (left column) and the parallelism to this book's chapter list (middle column).

Reference: https://en.wikipedia.org/wiki/The_Art_of_War

The Art of War chapter names in English translations	*The Art of Integrating Strategic Planning, Process Metrics, Risk Mitigation, and Auditing*		Page
Laying Plans	Chapter 1	Vision	3
The Challenge	Chapter 2	First Define Vision; Then Develop Strategic Plan	9
Strategic Attack	Chapter 3	Strategy: Measurement of Effectiveness Through Initiatives	17
Tactical Dispositions	Chapter 4	Initiatives to Support Strategies: Measurement through Process Metrics	23

List of Examples

List of Figures and Tables

Preface

The author's lessons learned—during more than 25 years of hands-on quality management experience in environments including manufacturing, medical devices, military, aerospace, automotive, and logistics—are condensed in this book to provide reference material to both beginners and seasoned professionals in the development and sustainability of an effective quality and operational system.

Experiences shared in this book include the design from ground zero-to-deployment, risk mitigation, and maintenance of quality standards such as ISO 9001, AS9100, ISO/TS 16949, TL 9000, FDA/GMP and C-TPAT standard, and Lean Six Sigma principles.

The main focus of this book is to promote the use of the internal auditing tool as a feedback mechanism not only for compliance verification but also for the measurement and enhancement of the system's effectiveness. The catalysts for this goal are:

- Auditing beyond compliance to include identification of improvement opportunities
- Use of process metrics as feedback mechanism in the discovery of hidden factories and risks

This book's scope extends to the main driver of the audit goal, which is the company's vision and strategic planning. The understanding and alignment of initiatives to the vision and strategic plan are critical in the overall success of the organization. This book will provide models and templates for the easy translation of these seemingly abstract guiding principles into easy to understand operational tasks.

Concepts and models discussed in this book are clearly illustrated using anonymous real-life examples encountered in day-to-day operations. These examples include lessons learned associated with compliance, continuous improvement, and techniques in the conversion of performance metrics as process indicators, savings' generators, and risk mitigation. These examples are simple and easy to understand and include templates for quick application with details on the creation of problem statements, root cause analysis methods, and design of action plans with measurement of success.

This book also highlights the implementation of models to help transform compliance audits into a more dynamic tool to generate continuous improvement, risk assessment, and measurable savings. This transformation will increase the visibility of the internal audit's added value to the organization and will further promote a unique partnership with the rest of the organization toward a common goal. This concept is shown in Figure 0.1.

In order to achieve this joint venture (i.e., beyond compliance and beyond sustainability), it is important that the team understand the integration and conversion of the vision, strategic plan, and departmental initiatives into common measurements as a feedback mechanism to the systems' continued compliance, improvement, and cost savings. The vibrant energy emanating from the process metric can be further optimized through the adaptation of these verifiable results into action. The internal audits' existing elements—such as root cause analysis and verification steps—may be applied to drill deep into the core issues beyond compliance. A relevant material reference is the author's earlier book, *Auditing Beyond Compliance*, published by ASQ Quality Press.

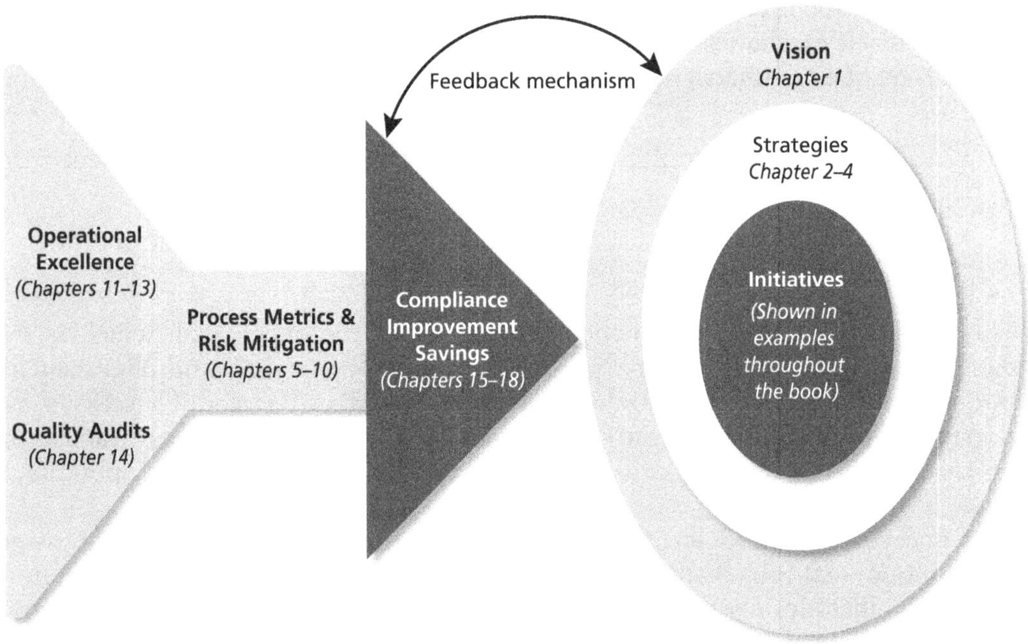

Figure 0.1 Model: Integration of strategic planning, risk mitigation, process metrics, and auditing.

This book provides models and application tools to simplify the translation of vision and strategies for the different levels of the workforce. Understanding these two high-level elements is the first step in the development and integration of initiatives to support an effective quality management system and operational excellence. This book also shows the interrelationship of root cause analysis, risk assessment, auditing, and process metrics in the alignment and measurement of initiatives with strategic planning. Low-hanging fruit is good to pick only if it is the desired fruit. This book will show the roadmap needed to pick the right fruit as the dynamic initiatives are critical in the continuing growth of the company, workforce, internal process development, and customer satisfaction.

What Does the Book Offer as Immediate Added Value?

- **Challenge Run**—Ideas outlined in this book offer immediate integration of the company's vision and strategies to help process owners quickly develop initiatives and process metrics without any capital expenditure, using only simple quality tools (templates provided). The last chapter presents a Challenge Run Starter Kit as a roadmap for the immediate implementation of models in the development or measurable initiatives. The author's experience included working with companies who had accomplished this endeavor in two to three months timeline. This is the challenge!
- **Models**—Models depicted in this book are easy to implement with examples showing real business scenarios (hidden identity) and tools proven to achieve measurable success. Models are simple and able to be customized for replication for any business type.
- **Workshop Modules**—There are also simple to deploy workshop modules showing how to use basic lean tools for industry problem solving and measurement of actions. These workshop modules may be used for reference or for group training on the lean tools. There is no need to have Lean Six Sigma certifications to implement these modules.

This book is divided into five parts to highlight the core business elements with significant impact on the company vision:

- Part I – Strategic Planning
- Part II – Process Metrics and Risks Mitigation
- Part III – Root Causes
- Part IV – Auditing
- Part V – Integration of Strategic Planning, Process Metrics, Root Causes, and Auditing

Each of the core elements is important not as a single entity. Combined, they function as an integrated unit to achieve quality beyond compliance and sustainability.

Acknowledgements

I want to offer a special acknowledgment to ASQ management and Quality Press staff for their hard work, professionalism, and fantastic support in helping me complete this project.

ASQ's various educational programs and knowledge enhancement activities, such as tutorial workshops and conference presentations, provided opportunities to share my experience and expertise, as well as to continually replenish my knowledge base from the ASQ community.

Special thanks to the following:

- Joy Hannan, Vice President of the Hoerner Company, for her support and confidence in my work.
- Shawn Masters, Chief Commercial Officer at ProTrans, for encouraging my continued participation in ASQ professional activities and giving me the support and opportunity to implement lean concepts and projects in the work environment.
- Purdue University TAP team, for giving me the opportunity to teach workshops based on my book, *Auditing Beyond Compliance*, as part of the University's community outreach program. Purdue University's support of my work gave me another perspective of lean implementation through the educational system.

PART I
Strategic Planning

1
Vision

The company vision should be the pivot point for all strategic planning, risk identification, and tactical deployment to ensure that major initiatives are aligned with stakeholder goals. This is like the starting point of a race, wherein the race teams follow the designated path—including the rules governing the race—to achieve the desired goal (that is, reaching the finish line). The vision should set the overall business goals or direction so that the strategic path and deployment can be *built, monitored,* and *measured* by the process owners with consideration of the risks involved.

The company vision should be the nucleus of the strategic business plans; otherwise, operational initiatives will likely drift off the desired target—a wasteful use of resources!

The vision is like the sail that guides the boat to its desired destination. Without the sail, the boat will be floating aimlessly without direction.

This chapter focuses on providing a roadmap for identifying the vision's core elements to help convert this seemingly inert concept into actionable and measurable results at all phases of the company.

CORE ELEMENTS OF THE VISION

The company vision steers the company to the desired business direction with minimum or acceptable risk. Without the vision, there is no guidance to align initiatives towards a common goal. Once the vision is defined by top management and understood and embraced by the workforce, the journey to reach the company goal can begin.

To begin this journey, it is imperative to first understand the core elements of the vision; without these core elements, the vision remains a static component of the business.

Many business practitioners may define these core elements differently, depending on the intended focus. This book focuses on a system with continuing verification and measurement throughout the different phases of the business to ensure alignment with the vision. Based on these objectives, this book defines the core elements as:

- **Strategic planning** ***(deployment of initiatives)***
- **Verification of effectiveness** ***(audit beyond compliance)***
  - Sub-elements of this core include the integration of the audit program in the periodic monitoring of the initiatives through compliance verification and identification of continuous improvement.
- **Measurement of success** ***(process metrics)***

  The two sub-elements are:
  - Performance level comparison against the expected results and progress towards the goal.
  - Control of risks to a minimum or acceptable level reflected by the tolerance (i.e., goal) built into the metrics.

Why choose these three components as the core elements above all other elements? These three elements epitomize the dynamics of a business cycle starting from the creation of the roadmap to reach the goal. This is a continuous flexible cycle, subject to re-adjustment to remain effective and within the bounds of the vision.

Once the vision is fully understood by the workforce, strategies and initiatives are easier to define. As one scholar said, *"you cannot reach your destination if you do not know where you want to go."* In other words, integration of strategies, initiatives, and metrics is key in achieving the company vision as shown in Figure 1.1.

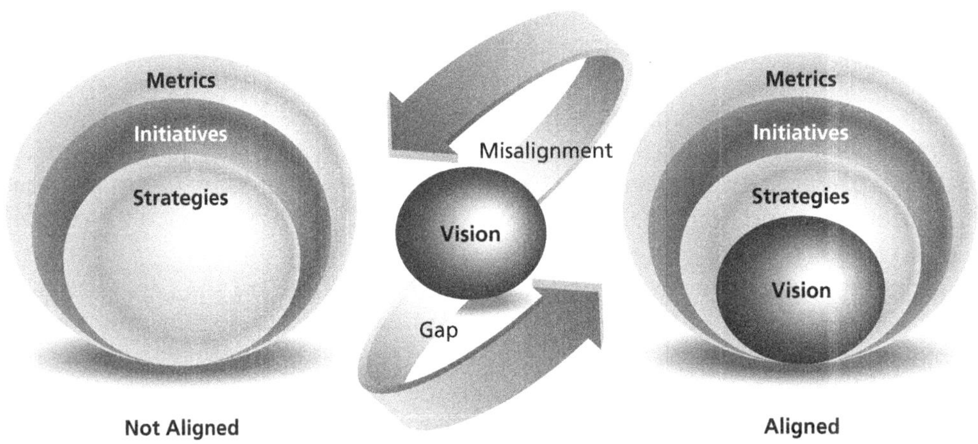

Figure 1.1 Misalignment of strategies and vision; evaluate/resolve gaps to ensure alignment of the elements.

Reference: "Checks and Balances – A technique to sync organizational vision and strategy," authored by Janet Smith and published in *Quality Progress,* August 2014.

http://asq.org/quality-progress/2014/08/back-to-basics/checks-and-balances.html

CRITICAL FACTORS INFLUENCING DEVELOPMENT OF VISION

Defining the vision is the responsibility of management. Depending on the size and structure of a company, the creation or revision of an existing vision may involve a multi-functional team authorized in the development of the business plan. The simplicity of the vision is critical in translating the business goals into a practical strategic plan and deployment programs that can be easily understood by the different tiers of the organization. An abstract, too complex, or vague vision will just add another layer of confusion and difficulty in developing aligned strategies to achieve the expected results. During the initial creation or modification of the company's vision, it is important to answer these key questions:

"Where are we now?"

"Where do we want to go?"

"What do we need to do to go to where we want to be?"

These simple questions will help identify the path for the company's business direction. There are many influencing factors in the creation of a vision, such as:

- Customer requirements or market trends
- Financial elements
- Competition or risks associated with the business
- Technology constraints
- Skill set of the workforce
- Regulatory governance
- Social responsibility

The selected influencing factors will be the business drivers in the development of the company's strategies to achieve the vision. The workforce's embrace of the vision is crucial in the creation of dynamic strategies and initiatives leading to the realization of the vision. A simple and clear vision statement with three core elements (Figure 1.2) has a higher probability of a successful deployment as there is lesser chance of misinterpretation by the workforce.

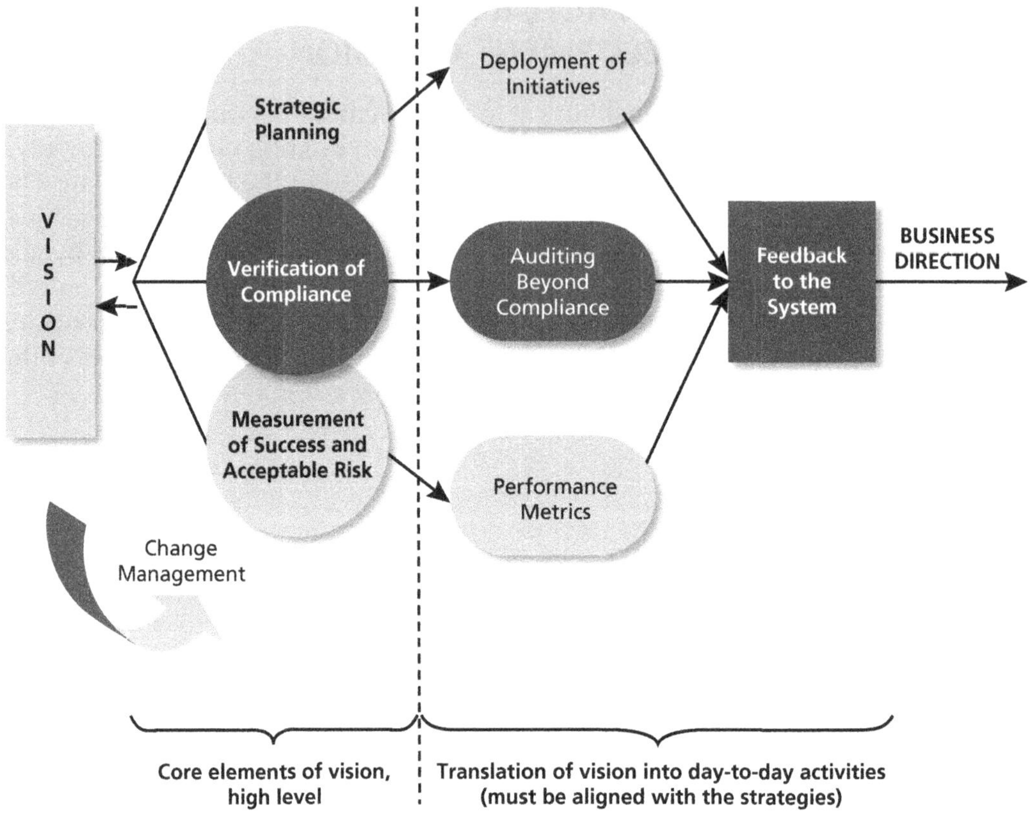

Figure 1.2 Core elements of the vision model.

Core Element: Strategic Planning

Strategic planning sometimes fails to provide a clear roadmap so initiatives can be effectively developed to support the objectives. Why? The developers of the strategic plan may not have involved key stakeholders to provide input in the practical deployment of the plan throughout the different phases of the business. Designing a strategic plan and actually executing the plan to meet stakeholder expectations are two different aspects of strategic planning. These initiatives possibly require multi-functional teams with varied expertise to support the successful completion of each phase. It is similar to surveying a piece of land for building a house. The construction design may look outstanding on the drawing board, but the chosen site may not be suitable for building (such as in a flood zone) if risk was not fully assessed. The strategic plan's deployment requires validation with consideration to influencing elements including the 'invisible' factors such as process owner buy-in. Without the buy-in element, the plan's deployment may encounter roadblocks and possibly deteriorate.

Core Element: Verification of Effectiveness (Auditing Beyond Compliance)

The successful deployment of a strategic plan does not mean completion of the plan. Once deployed, the plan still needs continuing verification to ensure its alignment with the vision and effectiveness in meeting the objectives. Auditing, a typical element of the quality and operational system, can be further optimized as the verification mechanism for compliance and beyond—such as the verification of initiative alignment and identification of continuous improvement opportunities. After all, these elements contribute to strengthen the grassroots of compliance!

Core Element: Process Metrics – Measurement of Success, Acceptable Risk, or Failure

Without any measurement against a benchmark, it is difficult if not impossible to judge current state or progress achieved. Performance metric is a feedback mechanism, an indicator to show the status of an initiative at any given time.

Each primary initiative supporting the vision and strategy is an active element that may behave as though it has a 'life of its own' once deployed. If not monitored and measured, these elements may stray away from the desired direction; thus it is imperative that a monitoring system start at the planning phase and continue through the deployment phase. This is accomplished through the installation of performance metrics at strategic points throughout the system. As discussed in later sections, it is imperative that the right metrics are measured in order to get the correct information needed to achieve the expected results.

In simpler terms, the vision is like the goals of an athlete. If the goal (vision) is to be an Olympic runner in the next four years, the plan to achieve this goal is laid out over this period of time. The plan may include the exercise regimen and training program (strategies) to build the vitality, stamina, and speed needed to achieve the goal. These strategies are divided into daily or weekly programs (initiatives) to measure progress (performance metrics). Completion of each daily or weekly program is monitored, measured, and compared (benchmark) from the previous results to determine improvement. Measurements of many variables at a set frequency (audit program) may include: run rate (miles/hour), pulse rate, blood pressure reading, and other indicators to assess readiness. Based on the measurements, certain influencing elements may be adjusted (change program) to optimize results, such as diet, length, and method of the exercise program or the severity level of the training program.

In a nutshell, the example above resembles a typical business flow, starting from the creation of the vision, strategic planning and deployment of initiatives, and auditing of compliance and effectiveness through the measurement of performance metrics.

2

First Define Vision; Then Develop Strategic Plan

Strategic planning is sometimes perceived as a silver bullet that will be the universal solution; in many cases, the result is a failed expectation as it is not totally understood by the workforce. *Why?*

Strategic planning has become a buzzword, giving the perception of a magic wand that will make stakeholder wishes come true. It can be that magic wand only if the holder will use this tool to its optimum power. This is not an unrealistic goal if the roadmap to this program is defined, understood, and supported by a closed loop system that runs between management and the grassroots level of the organization (Figure 2.1).

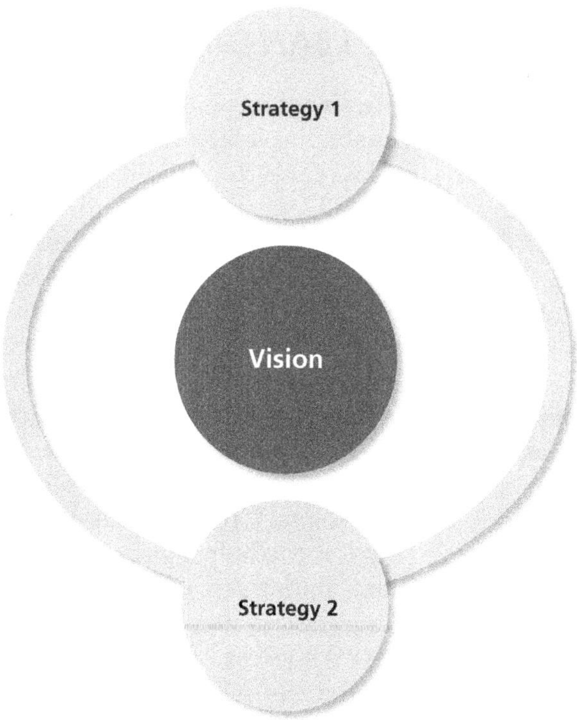

Figure 2.1 Strategies built around the vision model.

LIFE CYCLE OF THE STRATEGIC PLAN (DMAIC MODEL)

In the creation of a strategic plan, defining the vision's requirements will be the first task. Clear understanding of the vision will be key to the survival of an effective strategic plan. For example, if the vision states, *"company revenue growth by at least 50% in five years through business acquisition,"* what does it mean? Does it mean that stakeholders are planning to expand through the purchase of existing businesses? Are these businesses domestic or international? Is the acquisition limited to the same industry or different business types? These are just some of the critical questions that need clarification before strategies can be created to support the realization of the vision. Ambiguity of the vision statement will not only create confusion, but may also pose a difficulty in the formulation of pertinent strategies aligned with the vision. This is a common pitfall within the organization, wherein it is assumed that the workforce can easily formulate the operational strategies and initiatives to support the vision. Management can help increase the chances of realizing this expectation if the workforce is given some guidelines or tools to help the organization in formulating strategies aligned with the vision. How is this done? One method is the use of the lean DMAIC principle.

WHAT IS THE LEAN DMAIC MODEL?

DMAIC (define–measure–analyze–improve–control) is and a discipline that provides a methodology for analyzing a situation needing improvement or resolution (see Figure 2.2). In layman's terminology, this principle provides guidelines for unraveling the issue at hand with the ultimate goal of implementing a resolution using best practices in a streamlined fashion (through waste reduction).

There is nothing special or technical about the DMAIC concept; it is a common sense application of basic quality tools to define and achieve the set goal. The DMAIC principle is a technique or method of thinking applicable at any phase of the organization.

Alignment of strategies to the vision is not enough to ensure success. Strategies, per se, are lifeless as these elements do not have a self-supporting mechanism to sustain existence. In other words, strategies not implemented are like wall decorations, "nice to look at, but useless." Turning these strategies into working initiatives will serve as the driving force to help achieve the goal. Key performance indicators (KPIs) for the primary initiatives will provide visibility and early detection of success or failure.

Early detection of any initiative's success or failure is critical in analyzing the consistency of the results versus the desired outcome. The analysis phase will provide opportunity to uncover and mitigate anomalies impacting the desired results. Additional data mining may be required if available data do not provide conclusive evidence to support the desired outcome. It is not uncommon to

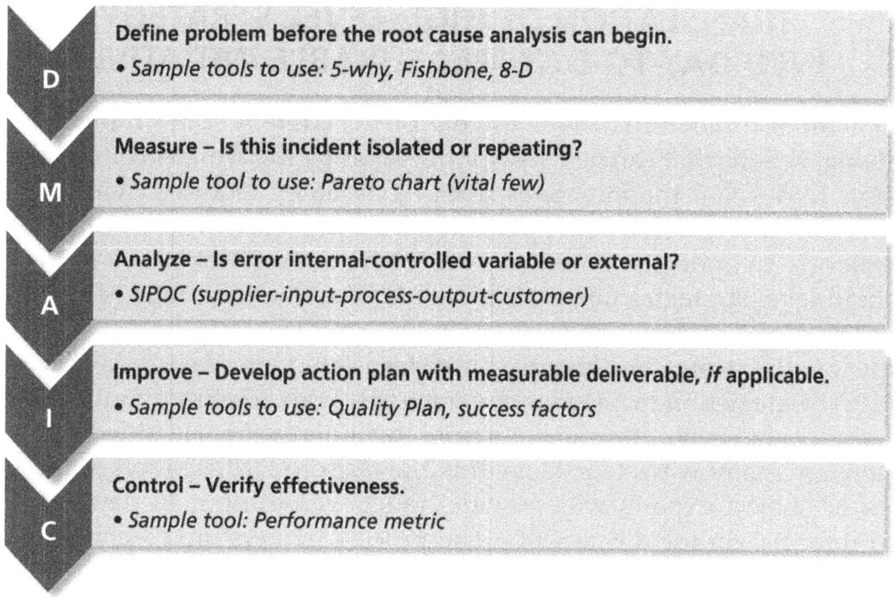

Figure 2.2 DMAIC methodology (define–measure–analyze–improve–control).

re-evaluate the vision statement at this phase of strategy planning (for example, at the discovery of unexpected variables beyond the organization's control, such as changes in the market trend or technology growth). Detecting major roadblocks at this point is better than discovering these variables at a later stage. Some analysis tools applicable for this stage are SIPOC (supplier-input-process-output-customer) and 5-why analysis.

Further breakdown of each strategy into initiatives is not enough to satisfy the vision. Strategy *per se* is abstract, sometimes overwhelming, and may sound like a philosophical concept that no one else understands except the initiator. Strategy needs to be translated into initiatives that can be easily implemented, measured, and owned by the workforce. These initiatives should be part of the day-to-day tasks embedded within the work instructions or policies. Translation of strategies into day-to-day operational tasks reinforces accountability and empowers the grassroots level in contributing to the successful realization of the vision. This can only be achieved by the process owners if there is clear understanding of the vision and strategy. One method of drilling down these expectations is to involve the workforce in the development of initiatives and performance metrics, such as the following example.

TRANSLATION OF HIGH-LEVEL STRATEGY INTO DAY-TO-DAY MEASURABLE INITIATIVES

It is sometimes difficult to convey the high-level strategy into simple day-to-day operational actions that can be easily understood by the workforce. The challenge for teams to develop the initiatives from the strategy requires creative thinking in looking at the big picture and dividing this big picture into smaller pieces for the workforce to understand and execute. There are multiple ways of translating these high-level strategies into operational levels. One technique is illustrated in Figure 2.3.

How are the strategies illustrated here translated into day-to-day measurable activities? Strategies, in most cases, are not easily converted into routine activities, which means that generating savings from the initiatives is an added challenge.

There are many ways to achieve this translation. Participation of the process owners or subject experts will provide added value input in data mining the related information for this activity. The process owners' involvement increases the buy-in and accountability in the execution of these initiatives.

Each initiative can be further broken down into sub-activities that will allow deeper drill down to expose other untapped sources of improvement opportunities. Once the initiatives are identified, the next step is the establishment of the benchmark *(where are we now?)* and goal *(where do we want to be?)*. The benchmark versus the goal will determine progress of the initiatives. Start simple.

Figure 2.3 Examples of strategies built around the vision.

Figure 2.4's matrix is one format to show how to execute an initiative through the identification of the requirements (success factors), desired output (deliverables) and metrics. The matrix shows the breakdown of the initiative and shows how the key criteria (success factors) selected by the process owners can be met as well as the measurement of these success factors. Because process owners have the knowledge and exposure to the major roadblocks needing improvement, their participation in the deployment of an initiative will be beneficial to the goal's success. The process owners may also have the 'solution' ideas that may help identify the performance metrics (that is, measurement of success factors). One can ask the process owner: "What roadblocks do you experience? And what changes would make your daily job easier?" These simple questions can help design the initiative.

Figure 2.4 depicts the streamlining of the document control process by identifying the success factors and the performance metrics for the measurement of success.

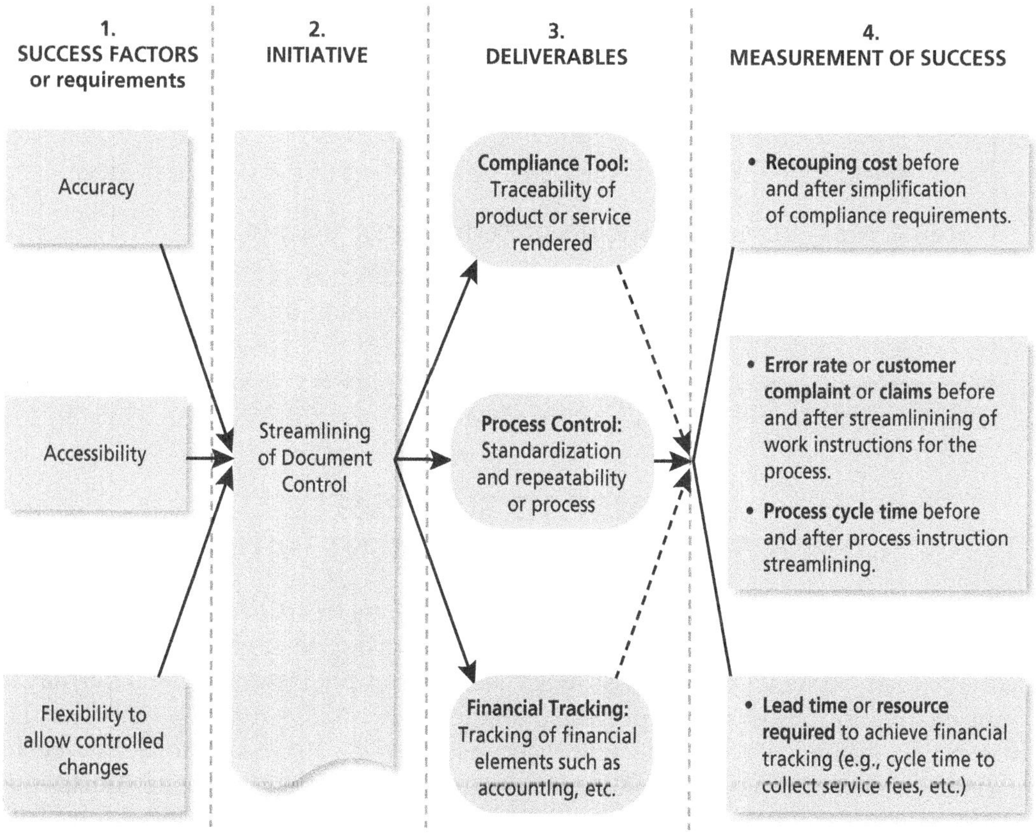

Figure 2.4 Matrix worksheet for the translation of high-level strategy into day-to-day measurable initiatives.

Example 2.1 Deployment of strategy: streamlining of document control program.

Outlined below is a step-by-step process for the translation of high-level strategy into day-to-day measureables as illustrated in Figure 2.4, a template that may be constructed and customized using the following steps:

Step 1. Success Factors or Requirements

List success factors needed to achieve the initiative. For this case, improvement of document control was the selected initiative.

The process owners chose three important success factors: accuracy, accessibility, and flexibility to allow controlled changes.

Step 2. Initiative

List the process or sub-processes involved in this initiative. In this case study, the process is document control.

Step 3. Deliverables

List expected results from this initiative important to the process owners.

Step 4. Measurement of Success or Performance Metrics

List pertinent metrics associated with the completion of the success factors; these need to be defined based on 'what matters' to the customer and stakeholders.

ROADMAP TO SUCCESSFUL STRATEGIC PLANNING—ALIGNMENT WITH VISION

The roadmap to successful strategic planning has many turns. Choices made lead to countless combinations of results, fueled by comparing desired expectations with realistic ones. Achievement of a strategy is not a simple quest and this journey's final destination may not be perfectly aligned with the mapped target (that is, vision, the primary driver). As with a travel plan, it's necessary to define basic variables before the start of a journey to ensure optimum alignment of efforts.

Strategic planning, as common as it may sound, has multiple definitions and scopes customized to its application. Unless the organization first defines the unique meaning of the strategic planning applicable to its system, there will never be a solid collaborative effort to sustain this initiative. It will be like an orchestra without a conductor to guide and merge all the musical sounds from the different instruments into one harmony. How do you define strategic planning that will best fit your organization?

The key word is *alignment*. It's necessary to align strategic planning with the company vision or business goal. Strategic planning that is isolated from or totally irrelevant to the company vision will never materialize. If it does, under this condition it will have a painful and short life cycle. How is strategic planning aligned with the vision? It is not always easy. This subject matter tends to be abstract; in some cases, it may even be philosophical in nature. One effective technique involves the creation of a tool, a model to simulate the process and lessen the ambiguity of the scope until it is fine-tuned to a manageable scale. The model or tool does not have to be complicated; it can be as simple as the creation of performance metrics that will reflect the success of the strategies' implementation. The operational initiatives to support these strategies should have relevant performance metrics to contribute to the strategies' end results.

Example 2.2 Alignment of strategies with vision.

A distributor of disposable medical devices wishes to align its company with the manufacturer providing the finished product. The manufacturer expanded its work hours to meet the increasing customer demand. The distributor envisioned that the increasing volume demand would also increase its revenue if the proper strategy were implemented. To maximize on this change, the distributor changed its vision to "increase the profit margin by 20% annually."

Two strategies were selected to achieve this vision:

- Strategy 1: Extension of work hours throughout the year to increase sales and profits.
- Strategy 2: Creation of on-line ordering process in addition to existing mode of order process.

One of the day-to-day initiatives to support the strategy was the staggering of worker hours during slow periods in order to minimize the need to hire additional personnel or to schedule overtime. Peak hours were identified to ensure full manpower support. To assess the effectiveness of the strategies and initiatives, the distributor created performance metrics shown in Figure 2.5 to control and monitor costs and profits. The simple matrix is monitored on a weekly basis through a structured internal audit by the team leaders to ensure compliance policies and procedures supporting the implementation of the day-to-day initiatives. The audit scope required auditing beyond compliance, which meant identifying and reducing day-to-day wastes associated with the process. Examples of wastes identified were excessive walking to retrieve parts for packaging, inaccessibility of packaging materials, and disorganization causing wasted time to search for right materials. These wastes were discussed and addressed after each audit. Improvement measurement is reflected in productivity metrics.

(continued)

Example 2.2 Alignment of strategies with vision *(continued).*

Performance	Actual Results	Benchmark	Goal
Monthly Sales and Profits	xx	Compare available data before and after the initiaitive	Goal should be achievable and reflect stakeholders' input
Daily Overtime	xx		
Productivity	xx		

Figure 2.5 Performance metrics matrix.

Lesson Learned

Any company's operational system should have the flexibility to implement changes needed to re-align with changing customer requirements (in this case, manufacturer's business direction).

Listening to the voice of the customer (VOC) to ensure alignment with the voice of the process (VOP) is necessary for continuous improvement. VOC and VOP tools include: customer surveys, correction action requests, internal audits, and management reviews.

Example 2.3 How do you align strategies when vision is blurred?

The director of engineering approached one of the company's executives and asked about scheduling a meeting to discuss the company's new vision for the coming year. The executive told the director that he had just discussed the vision with the lead engineer. The executive was on his way to the airport for an extended business trip to Mexico, so he asked the director to meet with the lead engineer about the new vision.

This example may sound ridiculous, but it is not uncommon. Sometimes a company's vision is 'just words,' with no substantial commitment from management.

It is management's responsibility to provide a clear vision drilled down to the workforce.

3

Strategy: Measurement of Effectiveness Through Initiatives

The effectiveness of a strategy is manifested at the different levels of the organization through the measurement of operational initiatives. It is important that performance measurements (success or failure rates) are installed at critical detection points to obtain incremental or accumulated values meaningful to the stakeholders. Interpretation of these measurements will be key in providing improvement feedback to the system and to input into assessing the strategies' effectiveness.

STARTING POINT

Selection of initiatives to support a strategy should involve the process owners' input to promote buy-in and integration of the lessons learned aspect. The process owners are the subject experts of their processes as they perform the tasks on a routine basis; this 'hands on' experience and knowledge base can be further optimized by tapping into this resource during the development of initiatives.

As these initiatives are translated into day-to-day operational activities, how do management and the grassroots level workers receive feedback if expected results are within or outside the goal? The creation of a continuing and structured performance metrics verification is the answer to this question. Incorporating the verification of the performance metrics in the internal audit program will not only help structure the metric periodic review but will also support the lean concept of auditing beyond compliance. Audit of an initiative's effectiveness seems vague and may sound too abstract. This is not the case; it is just like typical auditing except with the addition of some elements not necessarily included in routine auditing. The additional elements are success factors and the measurement of these success factors. Still sounds vague? It may be easier to explain this methodology through an example that includes the step-by-step creation of a matrix for measuring the effectiveness of strategies through initiatives (Example 3.1). This matrix can be made part of the document control or part of the audit checklist.

Example 3.1 Measurement of strategy effectiveness.

The matrix in Figure 3.1 shows one of the many methods used in measuring effectiveness of strategies through the performance metrics of the initiatives.

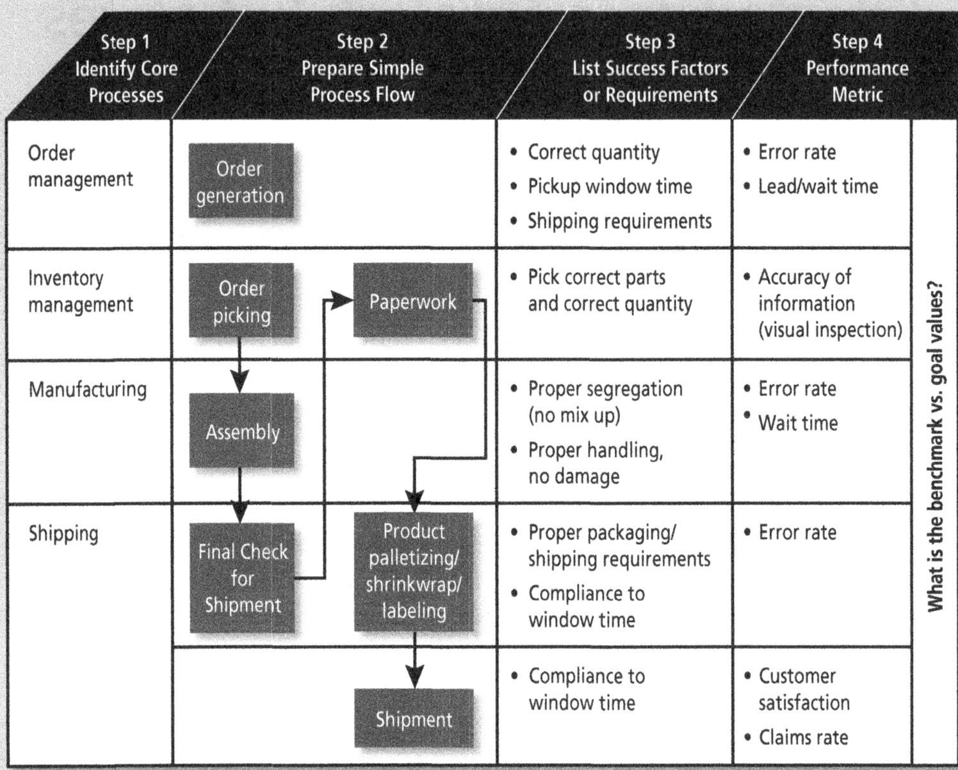

Figure 3.1 Matrix showing measurement of strategy effectiveness (through performance metrics).

Below are simple steps to convert Figure 3.1 into a customized template to verify the effectiveness of any operational initiative; it can be used during a periodic metric review or internal audit.

Step 1. Identify core processes

Not all processes are of equal importance in terms of risk and cost. For example, cycle time, skill set requirement, cost of resource (such as material), equipment involved with the process, bottleneck point, and other critical criteria may impact stakeholder requirements.

Step 2. Prepare a simple flowchart

Flowcharts help you visualize the integration and relationship of the process elements as well as the current flow and the ideal flow. The flowchart also helps expose wastes or non-added-value activities such as redundancies.

Step 3. List the success factors or requirements

Identification and visibility of the critical-to-quality (CTQ) factors for each core process and sub-processes are important to ensure success factors are integrated within the process.

Step 4. List measure of effectiveness for each process and sub-process

The metrics should be selected based on stakeholder interest. Measurement of the selected metrics will provide a mechanism for early detection of potential risks or failures so timely mitigation or action plans can be implemented.

In cases where a performance metric is composed of multiple sub-metrics, it may be beneficial to design a layered metric, discussed in the next chapter, to help ensure a balanced scorecard.

Note: List goals for each measurement and compare with the results. Root cause analysis or an action plan may be required to address significant gaps.

The monitoring of performance metrics may be at the overall system level or at a departmental level, such as in the example below. A structured performance metric may be designed to drill down to an individual employee's performance level as needed. The format depends on the visibility and details required to follow up an initiative's progress.

Example 3.2 shows the Quality Assurance department's initiatives to support the vision and the company strategy listed on the template Figure 3.2. This template may be used during periodic team review or can be made part of the scheduled internal audit checklist. The behavior of performance metric results—such as negative trends, fluctuating variation, or inactive state (no progress)—should prompt a root cause analysis to uncover the problem, if any, so that a proper action plan may be implemented. The internal audit is instrumental in the independent verification of the performance metrics' progress in addition to the assigned team reviewing the results on a scheduled basis. Corrective action may not only be limited to a compliance requirement, but may also include adjustment of the initiative or re-alignment of the goal. An effective audit root cause analysis has a significant role in the ultimate realization of the company vision.

Example 3.2 is a simple matrix showing the vision, the supporting strategy, and the departmental initiatives that include success factors and measurement. This storyboard may be used as a customized template for other initiatives. Results from each review period may be displayed as a trend chart for easy visibility of the historical data pattern.

Example 3.2 Translation of strategy into departmental-level initiative.

The effectiveness of a departmental initiative to support vision and strategy can be measured through performance metrics. Figure 3.2 is a simple matrix showing the translation of strategies at a departmental-level initiative.

A. Mission	B. Strategy	C. Initiatives	D. Actions/Deliverables (not limited to this list) List responsible name/timeline	E. Departmental Metric (Measure of success)	F. Progress
"Be one of the leading quality manufacturers of Product X in the next 3 years"	Develop a quality program to measure *compliance* and *continuous improvement*	Initiative 1: Implement sustainable quality audit program with compliance measurement	• Identify core process flow • Develop audit plan to evaluate compliance of core quality elements such as: management review, document control, customer focus, etc. • Develop audit checklist based on auditing beyond compliance	Compliance metrics for core areas: • Internal error rate • External error rate (e.g., claims, customer complaints)	Benchmark vs. goal?
	Success factor: Measurable and verifiable compliance, effectiveness of the quality system and improvement	Initiative 2: Implement a continuous improvement partnership between quality and operations through *auditing beyond compliance*	Project management plan to include: • Create VSM (value stream map) for all core processes to identify and prioritize opportunities • Develop process performance metrics measurement for each core process, such as process streamlining, waste reduction, resource optimization, etc. • Develop change management program	Improvement metrics: • Labor/material savings or utilization • Productivity • Process capability improvement • Waste reduction	

Figure 3.2 Simple matrix showing the translation of strategies at a departmental level initiative.

BENCHMARK VERSUS GOAL

The template illustrated in Figure 3.2 is a good reference point to quantify the seemingly abstract task of measuring strategy effectiveness. There is another challenge to using this model or template successfully—that is, deciding on the source of data for benchmark comparisons and for values to assign for goals. Some may say, *"Just do it; assign arbitrary numbers and adjust along the way."* Is this a practical approach? Probably, if this concept is applied on non-critical issues, or if cost is not an issue, or if time is not a factor to the stakeholders. However, this approach may pose high risk and possibly lead to loss of business if applied on critical items such as medical devices or other products or services impacting safety or requiring a large investment. So, what is the right approach in the selection of benchmark and goal?

Benchmark Selection – *Precautions*

Benchmarking is another element that is commonly misunderstood in the organization. There is a notion that the 'current state' is the actual performance exhibited by the process or resources. But the current state visible to the system may display superficial data not truly reflecting the inherent process capability.

The following are some examples of benchmarking failure modes.

Benchmark potential failure mode:
Variables supporting the process, such as resource or equipment, may not be at optimum capability; therefore, using this superficial data as a benchmark will provide the wrong indication of progress. See Example 3.3.

Example 3.3 Beware of superficial data.

A machine that was not being properly maintained was detected during the internal audit sampling. As corrective action, the machine was put on its regular preventive maintenance frequency, which improved its performance by reducing equipment downtime. An independent material change initiative was underway at the same time frame this equipment maintenance program was changed.

The correction of the equipment maintenance non-compliance, independent of the material change initiative, gave the false impression that the overall process improved due to the material change. In reality, had the equipment been operating at its optimum capability, the process benchmark would have been rated differently.

Lesson Learned:

Data must be analyzed and interpreted properly; it may uncover a strong undercurrent.

Benchmark potential failure mode:
Interim or temporary process conditions may not reflect the true capability during routine operations, therefore should not be used a benchmark. See Example 3.4.

Example 3.4 Assessment of true capability for benchmarking.

Technical temporary helpers or consultants under the tight supervision of experienced engineers had been hired during the validation of a complex project to accelerate the hand-off process to the manufacturing team. Data from this period would not be representative of the system or resource skill set. Inadvertent use of this data set as part of the benchmark may cause gaps or potential failures of the performance metrics.

Lesson Learned:

The scenario described above is another form of a hidden factory. The initiator of the process change (for example the Engineering VP) may assign these highly skilled helpers (e.g., consultants) to monitoring the process 24/7 to ensure the success of the proposal without considering the sustainability of the process once handed off to Operations.

Benchmark potential failure mode:

Use of the competition's metrics as benchmark, which may not match the company's internal processes.

The competition's performance metrics, as tempting as it is to match or exceed them, are not always beneficial. Variables surrounding the competition's metrics are process-specific and it may not be practical to use them as benchmark for internal processes. The selected benchmark should be based on the internal capability to reflect a metric pertinent to the company's vision and strategy and not based on some random competitive company.

Selection of a benchmark value requires a careful analysis to ensure there is consistency or stability of data as reference for monitoring progress.

Goal Selection

Some of the goal drivers include:

- Management vision, direction of the company
- Competition
- Regulatory directives
- Economy
- Technology change
- Market trend
- Financial aspect

4

Initiatives to Support Strategies – Measurement through Process Metrics

LAYERED PROCESS METRICS

The creation of layered process metrics may be one of the solutions in increasing the visibility of the many interrelated components supporting the primary metric. Failure of one component may impact the ultimate goal. Considering just the final result of the primary metric (example, on-time delivery 85%) and disregarding the associated activities impacting this final number may be a missed opportunity in identifying the weak and strong links within the internal and external supply chain system.

How to Create Layered Process or Performance Metrics

This layering method is similar to a work breakdown wherein the components of a primary metric are identified to evaluate the role and impact of each component on the final goal. One challenge in using this method is the development of a simple flowchart showing the interrelated activities supporting the core process bearing the primary metric. This may sound complex, but it is really a simple and interesting task if the process under evaluation is understood. Another analogy for the metric layered method is a relay race. Each runner must perform to the optimum level to achieve the overall goal of winning the race. A sub-standard performer may critically impact the team's success unless the other members can compensate for the lost time. This may work on a one-time basis or for non-critical events, but not for long-term or critical events such as the Olympics. Each selected member in such events has a required minimum performance metric (such as speed or endurance) to increase the probability of the team's success. This concept is true with any process; not knowing the capability of each component supporting the primary metric is a potential failure or customer dissatisfaction waiting to happen. Therefore, it is a proactive approach to identify core interrelated processes and define the appropriate performance metrics. Sometimes, assignment of the layered metrics is triggered by a non-traditional element such as a failure event. In-depth analysis of a failure using basic quality tools or lean concepts may reveal an opportunity for a work breakdown and the creation layered performance metrics.

METHODS FOR CREATING A LAYERED PROCESS OR PERFORMANCE METRIC

There are several methods for creating a layered process or performance metric. This book will focus on the methodologies explained in the following pages and will make use of various examples. It is at your discretion to use the appropriate method, based on the objective and available information. The intent of showing these different methods is to expose the reader to different options and perspectives when developing or reviewing performance metrics.

Just because your Final Assembly Manager says, *"Productivity is good this week; it exceeds the goal and we did not hire additional people,"* it does not necessarily mean success. You must look at the scrap report, cost of replacement parts log, and overtime log before rejoicing on the news. Performance metrics, if designed properly, should be good indicators of the true health of the process. Periodic monitoring of the indicators by process owners and incorporating this periodic review in the audit program will likely double the strength of its value. Otherwise, data collection without a purpose is like data left in the server as wasted space.

Some methods for creating layered performance metrics:

- **Method 1:** Use of 5-why process as the foundation
- **Method 2:** Use of simplified quality plan
- **Method 2a:** Use of control plan (a branch of the quality plan)
- **Method 3:** Use of different influencing variables to calculate same metric
- **Method 4:** Breakdown of process input and output

If the layering breakdown of the performance metric or the reporting format is not useful, change the format to fit user needs.

The following are some examples explaining the different methods for creating layered performance metrics using basic lean tools.

Example 4.1 Use of 5-why analysis as the foundation.

A 5-why analysis of a problem identifies an opportunity in creating a layered performance metric. The performance metric for each step uncovered in the 5-why analysis was developed by identifying the success factor needed for each step that could have avoided occurrence of the failure.

Problem statement: This month's on-time metric is 85%.
On time delivery metric goal: 100%
Find: Root cause

Using the 5-why analysis, the following information was uncovered.

Why 1: **Why was the on-time delivery metric not 100%?**
Because the delivery windows were not met.

Success factor needed for this step:
Delivery window time versus actual delivery cycle time

Metric for this step (1st layer):
Success rate in meeting delivery window time

Why 2: **Why were the delivery windows not met?**
Because Operations did not get the raw materials needed for the order on time.

Success factor needed for this step:
Material availability when needed

Metric for this step (2nd layer):
Material inventory or material planning accuracy (demand versus availability)

Why 3: **Why was the raw material not released on time to Operations?**
Because there was a delay in the release of re-ordered correct material.

Success factor needed for this step:
On-time release of material to Operations

Metric for this step (3rd layer):
Compliance to material release cycle time

Why 4: **Why was the material re-ordered?**
Because the wrong material was ordered, causing a delay in the release of the correct material.

Success factor needed for this step:
Accuracy of material order information

Metric for this step (4th layer):
Frequency of re-ordered material due to material demand list error

Why 5: **Why was the wrong material ordered?**
Because Inventory Control repeatedly gave the wrong material demand to Planning

Success factor needed for this step:
Inventory accuracy

Metric for this step (5th layer):
Accuracy and timeliness of material planning

Lesson Learned:

The different processes directly impacting the on-time delivery metric need to have performance metrics or requirements to support the primary metric (i.e., on-time delivery). This breakdown method will help identify the failure driver or potential risk so proper actions may be taken. It should be noted that the creation of the layered metrics is based on the practicality of the situation; each step does not have to have metrics, and a procedural requirement may suffice in some cases.

In the example above, the drill-down analysis of the on-time delivery metric led to the breakdown of the chain of events that led to the failure of not meeting the shipment requirement. Each response to the 5-why analysis in the example above can be converted into a performance metric (i.e., layered metrics) for the associated core processes as indicators. As these metrics are developed, focus on areas needing improvement (vital few) will be highlighted to help ensure the overall effectiveness of the system.

Existence of layered performance metrics would have triggered an early detection of potential failures or risks. In this example, it is the faulty inventory control method of identifying material demand that affected the on-time delivery metric—a hidden sub-element of the on-time delivery. Deterioration of a process metric does not happen overnight. If monitored properly, early intervention of the symptoms may be possible to prevent failures.

Example 4.2 Use of layered process metric.

Figure 4.1 shows an example of a layered performance metric regarding on-time delivery. The matrix shows the breakdown of the interrelated processes and the success factors for each (layered metrics) process that need to be fulfilled to achieve the overall expected metric (i.e., on-time delivery).

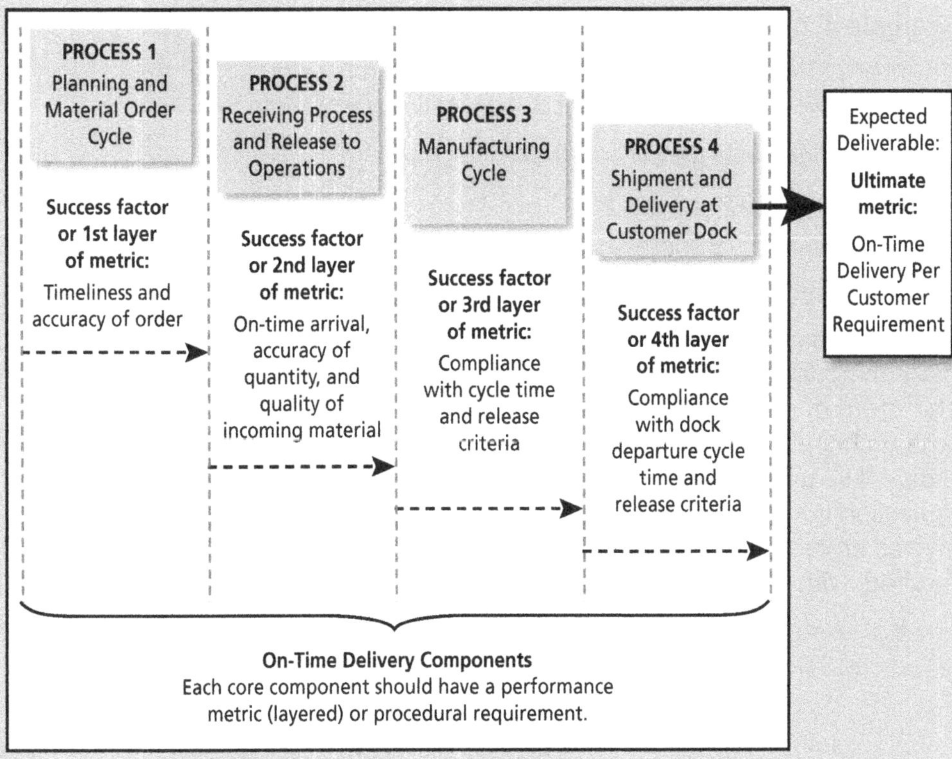

Figure 4.1 Layered process metric example: on-time delivery.

Meeting the success factors or acceptable risks for each supporting process will result in meeting the ultimate metric (e.g., on time delivery).

Review of any process metric may also reveal 'isolated incidents' wherein the root cause is an outlier and not a reflection of the overall performance level. Outliers, typically, have special causes and may not require an action plan (for example, delay due to hurricane). A contingency plan for addressing outliers may be more appropriate in some cases (e.g., alternate plan for power outage).

Do all processes require performance metrics? No. Not all supporting processes require a performance metric to ensure fulfillment of the overall process success; in some cases, procedural requirements and proper training of the process owners may be sufficient, especially if there are process controls in place to counter-check the activities. The decision to create a performance metric at a certain operational phase is at the discretion of the company based on many factors—resource availability, risk involved at certain points, cost effectiveness, and others.

Example 4.3a Use of simplified quality plan.

Another method for creating a layered metric is to develop a high-level quality plan showing an overall picture of the operational elements such as:

- Interrelated activities or sub-processes
- Responsible process owners
- Requirements or success factors or potential risks for each component, and
- Process metrics to measure these requirements against a goal.

This method provides more details on sub-process interactions and controls in place that may be applicable in certain operational decision making situations. The depth of details for this model depends on the company's need. In most cases, a high-level approach will provide more flexibility to the users. Too much 'noise' (i.e., unnecessary information) may interfere with the analysis, causing deflection from the original intent of the activity. The concept of creating the layered process metrics discussed above remains the same for this second method, with the addition of more information about the process.

See this example expressed in a matrix showing layered process metrics based on a condensed quality plan in Figure 4.2.

Process Owners	High-level Process Flow	Success Factors (Requirements)	Control in Place	Performance Metric (measure of effectiveness)
Planners	Order generation → Paperwork	• Customer specification • Quantity • Compliance with cycle time	Open order log checked daily	Error rate Cycle time
Quality	Material picking from inventory/ release to production	• Pick the right product, right quantity, and comply with proper handling	Quality release inspection report – per order	Accuracy (freight vs. paperwork)
Production/ Quality	Production processes	• Compliance with work instructions and process parameters	Completed lot report	First pass yield Error rate Cycle time
Quality	Preparation for shipment	• Compliance with packaging specifications	Quality release inspection report – per order	Error rate (freight vs. specification) Freight integrity (no damages)
Shipping	Shipment to customer	• Compliance with shipping specifications	Completed lot report	On-time delivery with correct quantity, intact freight delivered to the right customers

Figure 4.2 Layered process metric example: high-level quality plan.

Trending of these components will serve as feedback to the different process owners on how their performance metrics impact the overall goal. Understanding of their day-to-day operational metrics will serve as their roadmap in ensuring alignment with the company strategies and objectives.

How in-depth should each component be subdivided for an effective process measurement? The level of component breakdown may depend on the following factors:

- Complexity of the process
- Risk associated with the related activities
- Cost effectiveness of the data collection and the added value of the data

One guiding principle for this activity is to first identify the critical factors to success (what are we trying to achieve?) to create the 'boundaries' in staying focused on 'what really matters' to the stakeholders, based on a Balanced Scorecard.

Note: The Balanced Scorecard model considers the interest of the customer, financial aspect of the company, learning and growth of the workforce, and internal processes.

Examples of critical factors to success include:

- Customer satisfaction
- Company's continued profitability
- Company's recognition in the industry
- Internal process growth and competitiveness
- Continuing mitigation and control of risks to a minimum or acceptable level
- Workforce development
- Marketing leverage
- Social responsibility (such as environmental initiatives)

Example 4.3b Use of the control plan to break down processes, critical-to-quality-of-success factors, and corresponding process metrics.

What are the benefits of using the control plan format for capturing and monitoring the process metrics?

The control plan format is an accepted industry format in most business types such as medical device, automotive, military, and other commercial manufacturing industries. There are several variations of this format, but the concept remains the same as shown in Example 4.3a, reflected in a control plan format. This document may be adapted to any type of industry and may be used on a high-level system or to a specific process. The creation of this document sometimes involves not only the internal process owners' input but may also require the customers' feedback to accurately reflect the voice of the customer. The control plan, just like any other document, is a 'lifeless, no-added-value' piece of information unless it is used as a feedback mechanism to the system. How?

It can be used as part of the audit system checklist and part of the routine performance review metrics (independent of the audit system). These two 'touch points' should help in the timely detection of any trend or significant deviation from the goal. These two structured programs (i.e., inclusion in the audit checklist and in routine performance review) should increase the visibility of the performance metrics as a dynamic added-value mechanism.

Use a condensed control plan to identify process parameters, success factors, and process metrics to measure achievement of the requirements. The example in Figure 4.3 is a simple, condensed version of a control plan that may be used as a template with modification to fit the user's specific criteria.

CONTROL PLAN
(Condensed version)

Process: Raw Materials – Quarantine – Stockroom	Team:
Revision/Effective Date:	

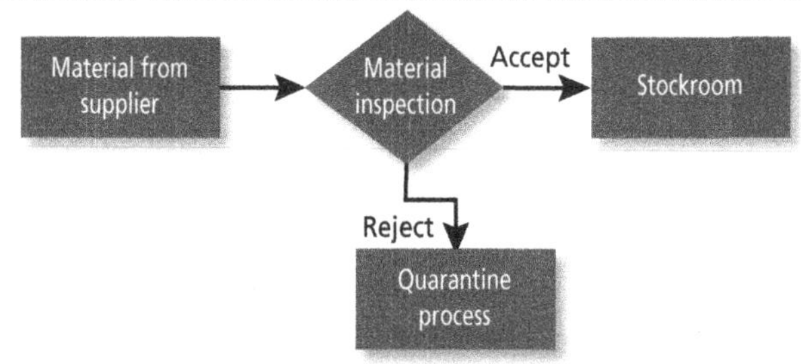

Process	Requirements or Success Factors	Method of Measurement	Method of Control	Process Metric	Reaction
Raw material inspection	a. Zero defect: Compliance with material specifications XX and drawing XX	a. Visual inspection and dimensional measurement	a. Every lot inspection and QA approval of results-procedure XX	a. Lot acceptance rate b. Supplier conformance rating (accepted lots) ≥ 98% per review period	a. Technical review board recommends resolution b. Supplier rating program
Quarantine	XX	XX	XX	XX	XX
Stockroom	XX	XX	XX	XX	XX

Figure 4.3 Identification of a process metric using a control plan.

Example 4.4 Use of different influencing variables for the same metric.

Another form of layered process metrics is the reporting of the same metric using different influencing variables to calculate the final number. It is similar to the concept as discussed above, with emphasis on metrics that are important to the user. If there are, for example, multiple interrelated sub-processes with corresponding metrics, the process owner may choose to use just one of the metrics to highlight a point of interest.

A selected influencing variable may be chosen for the purpose of increasing the visibility of certain vantage points. What is the added value of this method? The visibility of the influencing variable helps direct the focus of the improvement plan to continually ensure the system's effectiveness. This method will also help facilitate an in-depth drill-down measurement of the supporting business units' performance level and the identification of improvement opportunities. Reporting just the final metric without consideration of the associated variables may sometimes hide the obvious culprit of a failure.

The system's growth and sustainability will be hindered by these hidden variables unless they are quantified and addressed. The chosen influencing variable may 'swing' the results to highlight elements that may be beneficial or biased, depending on the intent of data collection champion.

> *For example, a salesperson may have sold the service offering a shorter lead time than the operational capability. Therefore, late deliveries may not necessarily be due to operational issues, but due to an element committed to the customer beyond the operational scope. Reporting the on-time delivery metric into layers, such as inclusion of actual cycle time to process the orders versus the allotted lead time, will reveal this hidden root cause impacting on-time delivery.*

How can one prevent the report from being biased and an unbalanced measurement of the system? There are many ways to optimize the measurements and retain the neutrality of the results. Another method is the reporting of primary and secondary metrics to show counterbalancing of the results (such as productivity versus error rate). It is therefore critical that performance metrics are developed around the critical success factors that add value as a feedback mechanism to the system. Table 4.1 is an example of reporting the same metric using different influencing variables to calculate the final metric. In this case study, the metric under evaluation is the delivery performance.

Table 4.1 Use of different influencing variables: delivery performance metric.

Examples of influencing variables selected by process owners to calculate metric (i.e., delivery performance)	Calculation formula	Plan for improvement
(A) Total number of orders (B) Total number of orders delivered on promise date and in full quantity	***Measurement 1:*** Delivery performance to promise date % delivery on promise date and in full quantity = (B) / (A) x 100	*Plans should be developed to address trends focusing on the variables showing deterioration or improvement opportunities such as:* *– Negative on-time delivery trend* *– High credit adjustment trend versus volume, etc.*
(C) Total number of orders delivered on promise date but partial shipment	***Measurement 2:*** Delivery performance to promise date but partial % delivery on promise date but partial shipment = (C) / (A)x 100	
(D) Total number of orders delivered on promise date with price adjustments	***Measurement 3:*** Delivery performance with price adjustments % delivery on promise date with price adjustments = (D) / (A) x 100	

Example 4.5 Breakdown of process input and output: use of SIPOC concept.

Breakdown of the process input is another method of identifying the elements impacting the expected end result. Because there are several inputs for a process, it is important that the process owner and the stakeholders are involved in the selection of the vital few elements. Not everything has equal importance, with limited resources and time; it is cost effective and efficient to prioritize using standard criteria (e.g., prioritization by risk).

Verification of each input element other than compliance will help focus the root cause analysis to identify the existence of any gaps or failure to meet the ultimate customer expectation. How? Verification of the procedural requirements or process metrics associated with the elements will help narrow the analysis to the right direction.

Figure 4.4 shows process element breakdown using the SIPOC flow. SIPOC (supplier-input-process-output-customer) is a basic lean-based tool to help outline the process variables. The input/output elements are selected for evaluation based on the scope of the study. It is not unusual to add or remove input/output elements from the SIPOC flow as more information is uncovered during the analysis. The Pareto concept (selection of the vital few) may apply in the prioritizing of the elements to be evaluated, especially under resource or time limitation.

This chart may be customized to user needs as a lean-based template.

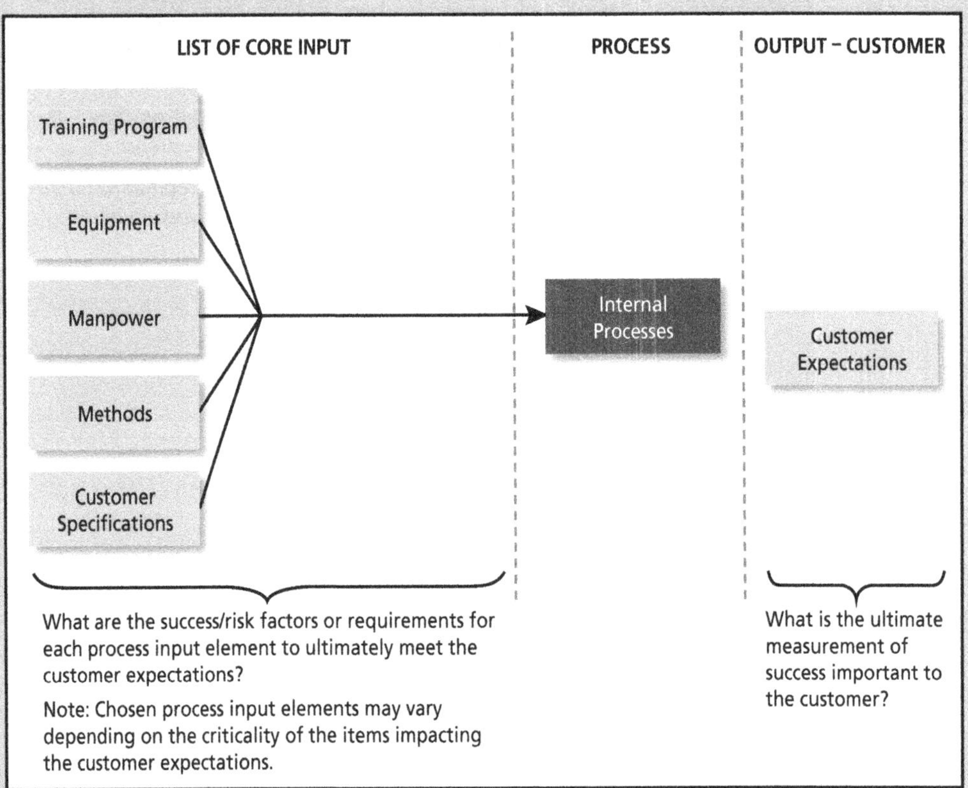

Figure 4.4 Breakdown of elements associated with a process using SIPOC flow.

PART II
Process Metrics and Risk Mitigation

5

Process Metrics and Risk Mitigation

FEEDBACK MECHANISM TO GO BEYOND COMPLIANCE AND SUSTAINABILITY

Process metrics, like the rails of a train track, ensure that the train moves within its bounds and acceptable risks. Without process metrics, initiatives may go in different directions and may fail to achieve the desired output directed by the vision and strategy. Process metrics, if selected carefully, are early indicators of vision and strategy alignment and permit the implementation of timely mitigation to prevent exceeding acceptable risks resulting in possible failures. In order for process metrics to work as the intended feedback mechanism to the system, the workforce must understand benefits and roadblocks.

PROCESS METRICS: SUCCESS FACTORS, RISK MITIGATION, FAILURE MODES, AND COUNTERMEASURES

Variables influencing performance metrics' effectiveness as indicators of process performance include:

- Recognition of the success factors (what is needed to make this work?)
- Identification of potential risks (control of risks and mitigation plan)
- Recognition of failure modes (knowing the roadblocks or failure modes aids in selection of solutions)
- Selection of best countermeasures to address roadblocks

The following are examples of performance metrics success factors, risk mitigations, failure modes, and countermeasures.

Process Metrics – Success Factor 1

There has to be a system for disseminating the vision and strategies to the grassroots level so the workforce has full understanding of the expectations.

Examples of Possible Failure Mode

- *Poor internal communication systems* inadvertently block the information from reaching the grassroots level; thus, workers may not be aware of management's expectations.
- *Internal silos* formed by inner circles to limit the flow of information to selected or favored groups are not uncommon; this practice is perceived by some as a source of power through the control of knowledge sharing. This behavior is beyond the control of anyone because this is an inherent work ethic; however, there are countermeasures to prevent such behavior in the organization, as mentioned below.

Examples of Possible Action Countermeasures/Risk Mitigation

Increase visibility and review of core metrics to help in the free flow of knowledge providing accessibility to all levels of the workforce:

- *Display core metrics,* such as communication board, internal newsletter, etc. This is one way to break the silos and the 'exclusive club membership.'
- *Set periodic review meetings* including the appropriate grassroots levels for early identification and mitigation of issues.
- *Provide feedback* on achievements as acknowledgement of individual and team progress (not just on failures).

Example 5.1 Breakdown of process input and output: use of SIPOC concept.

For example, one of the performance metrics for ABC Company's machining department is overtime cost. Salaried supervisors (who are not paid overtime) were pressured to work longer than their shifts because performance was measured against volume output without overtime. The department manager continued to meet (or even exceed) the resource allocation metric by using the supervisor time in lieu of hourly machine operators (to avoid overtime cost). When one of the supervisors left, the replacement was not willing to be continually used as 'free labor' and brought this practice to management's attention; the department manager's tactic collapsed.

Lesson Learned:

This is a classic example of sub optimization (i.e., waste of supervisor time) as well as an ineffective performance metric with no long-term sustainability.

An anomaly such as the one cited in this example may be uncovered with many techniques. One simple method is a time study of worker performance versus the required output due to volume and overtime trend. This should give a preliminary assessment of resource needs to initiate a more in-depth evaluation of the process variables.

Process Metrics – Success Factor 2

Selection criteria should be aligned with the vision and strategy.

Examples of Possible Failure Mode

Ineffective selection of metrics causing misalignment with the vision and strategy may be due to the following:

- *Inexperience or myopic perspective* of leaders in understanding the vision and strategy.
- *Intentional misguidance* of the metric system for personal gain by highlighting only successful metrics and disregarding metrics that show failures or inefficiencies or incompetence in the areas of responsibility (e.g., excessive overtime due to poor planning of resources with peak volume).
- *Changes may not be easily visible,* thus metrics initially aligned with the vision are no longer effective.

Examples of Possible Action Countermeasures/Risk Mitigation

- *Counter-balance metrics* should be implemented as applicable. There should be a secondary metric, if feasible, to measure the 'aftereffect' of the primary metric. These metrics need periodic review to determine any trending as the measurement behaviors may indicate variations or incremental changes in the system.

  For example, operational measures such as productivity should have a countermeasure metric, such as error rate, to minimize bias. The productivity metric of a process may not be as impressive if increasing manufacturing errors (not detected by internal process controls) reported by the end users are taken into account as part of the performance metric.
- *A change management system* should be in place to ensure proper validation, deployment, and monitoring of continuing effectiveness.

Example 5.2 Failure mode: lack of change management.

Company ABC's metric's goal for the inspection cycle should have been adjusted after the replacement of the manual inspection method with the automated optical inspection machine (i.e., shorter cycle). The new metric's goal should match (but not exceed) the optimum capability of the machine.

Lesson Learned:

Change management should be a living element to detect and capture major changes.

Performance Metrics – Success Factor 3

Consistent deployment structure of the initiative program throughout the organization.

Examples of Possible Failure Mode

Non-standard deployment methodology will likely cause various interpretations. Some of the core elements subject to variation unless defined are:

- Measurement method
- Scope and frequency of data collection
- Review process and/or audit process
- Change management
- Containment and escalation paths

Examples of Possible Action Countermeasures and Risk Mitigation

Methodology needs to be validated, standardized, and documented for repeatability and traceability. The elements identified in the failure mode above should be part of this validation to ensure the process owners' understanding of the tasks involved.

Example 5.3 Failure mode: scope of metric program not standardized.

The development of a customer satisfaction metric may consider only customer complaints requiring a formal corrective action as part of this metric; complaints received by Operations via telephone calls or email inquiries may not be captured if data collection scope is not clearly defined. It is not uncommon to hear 'it is not a complaint, the customer is just asking us to closely watch this issue, customer is not asking for a corrective action—case closed." This statement may be true, but the customer dissatisfaction associated with this inquiry may be a symptom of an incremental internal process variation slowly accumulating to erupt into a disaster. Or it may have been an isolated incident; the system will not know unless these dissatisfactions are recorded.

Lesson Learned:

Define and standardize the scope and methodology of the metrics program. If you don't, the program will be a waste of resources and no added value can be expected. The methodology should facilitate the recording of the VOC (voice of the customer) regardless of the reporting medium used by the customer. A more proactive approach is the gathering of customer feedback through a simple survey of customer perception.

Success Factor 4 – Periodic Review to Verify Continuing Alignment with Expected Results

Examples of Possible Failure Mode

Without structured review, system metrics will be stagnant. There is no real added value generated if metric measurement is not used as feedback to the process to trigger action.

It is not uncommon to hear the workforce say *"Why do we keep using this metric? Nothing is being done—it is a waste of time."*

Examples of Possible Action Countermeasures/Risk Mitigation

Periodic review of metrics should be structured as a visible support to the program. Metrics should be realistic and meaningful to the process owners.

> **Example 5.4** Periodic review of metrics.
>
> Company ABC used to perform the in-house calibration of machine X. For this task, the machine operators were required to record machine uptime, one of the calibration metrics. A year ago, calibration was outsourced and calibration variables were changed; some measurements were no longer applicable, including the monitoring of uptime hours. Machine operators kept on manually logging the uptime without knowing that this measurement had been made obsolete.
>
> **Lesson Learned:**
>
> A structured review of process metrics and communication system would have saved those operators time spent measuring and logging an obsolete metric. Incorporating the review of departmental metrics in scheduled internal audits will be another way of ensuring review of the initiative's effectiveness.

Process Metrics – Success Factor 5

Metrics should trigger an action plan or improvement.

Examples of Possible Failure Mode

Failure to initiate action or improvement may be due to one of two things:

- *Metric may no longer be applicable* due to various factors such as changes in the process, resource, environment, etc.
- *Metric may be too broad,* without the sensitivity needed to detect incremental variations of the sub-elements within the metric and therefore non-reactive to these changes.

Examples of Possible Action Countermeasures/Risk Mitigation
Periodic assessment of metrics alignment with the vision allows detection of incremental variation, and therefore early mitigation. One question should be asked: "What is the purpose of this metric; are the parameters for this metric still applicable"?

Example 5.5 Periodic assessment metric alignment.

Measurement of a broad metric, such as manufacturing lead time, is subject to various interpretations. This metric has several sub components—supplier compliance in providing acceptable raw material, effectiveness of workforce training to prevent internal errors, compliance to prevent machine downtime—that must be identified. Once the sub components are outlined, then individual performance metrics for each major sub component can be assigned to areas needing improvement.

Lesson Learned:

The breakdown of a primary metric into its core sub components will facilitate focusing on the problematic component impacting the overall metric. "Layered Process Metrics" as discussed in this book may be applicable for this situation.

Success Factor 6 – Measurement Should be Practical and Cost Effective

Examples of Possible Risk or Failure Mode
Known critical measurements may be inadvertently or purposely skipped due to various limitations, such as lack of resource, equipment, technology, etc.

Examples of Possible Action Countermeasures/Risk Mitigation
Alternate indicators should be considered in measuring critical metrics that are not easily visible.

Example 5.6 Performance trend: early warning indicators.

A stockroom manager of ABC Company was spending six hours per week manually calculating the process metric of the Receiving department to find out why materials were not being released to his department in a timely manner as they were in the past. The stockroom manager wanted to do a hidden study of the Receiving department's cycle time and practices to uncover the delay, so he did not want to ask the Receiving department about it. After a few months of study, the stockroom manager did not find anything out of the ordinary but was still wondering about the cause of the delay. Finally, the stockroom manager asked the new Receiving manager how the materials were being released. To the stockroom manger's surprise, he found that the delayed release was due to the outsource inspection of some of the materials. The customer had changed the test requirements and ABC Company had limited inspection equipment to match the new customer requirements; outsourcing the inspection was the option chosen. The delivery window had been changed to accommodate this extra step, but the stockroom manager was not aware of the change.

Lesson Learned:

The stockroom manager's wasted data collection effort could have been avoided, but an internal silo (i.e., prevention of free information flow) caused poor internal communication. The process metrics of material delivery would have made this change more visible to the process owners because the outsourcing change would have been reflected in the metrics.

6
Process Metrics – Why Do They Fail?

There are many reasons why process metrics fail. In most cases, failure has something to do with the alignment of process capability with stakeholder expectations. Failure of the metrics is not necessarily a reflection of the process performance. Failure may be due to other contributing variables that may or may not be easily visible to the process owners. Understanding the reasons for process metrics failure is critical in assessing the situation and risks in order to permit early detection and proper action. The following are some scenarios and examples describing these risks and failure modes.

RISK AND FAILURE MODE: PROCESS CAPABILITY AND CUSTOMER REQUIREMENTS MAY BE PERFECTLY ALIGNED, BUT PROCESS OWNERS ARE NOT

Perfect alignment of process capability and customer expectations does not guarantee successful metrics (see Figure 6.1). There are many dynamic variables surrounding the processes, and these variables need to be synchronized toward a common goal.

Process parameters with optimum setting are not immune to variations induced accidentally or intentionally, causing incremental deviations within the process. See failure mode examples that follow.

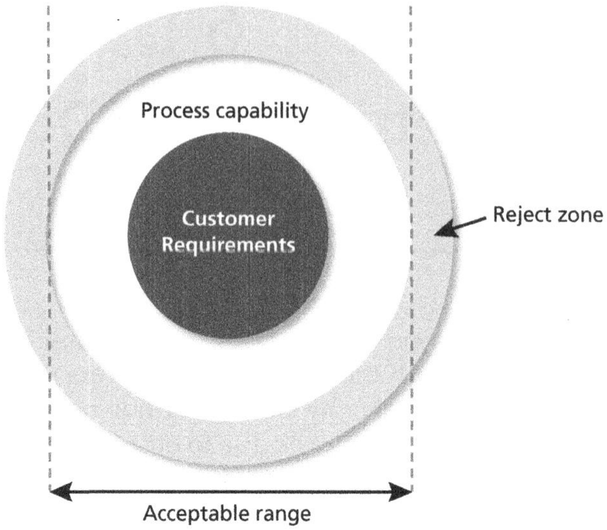

Figure 6.1 Risk and failure mode: process capability and customer requirement alignment.

Example 6.1 Alignment of process variables.

The Plating Manager miscalculated the resource allocation for an order and the customer had already signed the contract. The Plating Manager did not want to admit to the CEO that he needed ten plating operators instead of six. Under time and resource constraints, the inevitable happened—shortcuts, increasing risk, and probability of failure. The process owner's deviation from the approved processes (such as taking shortcuts) to meet operational requirements may have not been easily noticeable, but in time it will accumulate to show negative impact on the system.

Lesson Learned:

Information used for ensuring the success of a contract review should be under periodic validation. For example, time study of processes for resource allocation may require re-validation before a major contract is accepted. Process parameters do not remain static and changes such as material, skill set, complexity of the customer job, and other major process elements may have significant impact on the process cycle and resource requirement.

RISK AND FAILURE MODE: PROCESS IS BARELY CAPABLE

Barely capable process means that parameters are not stable and do not guarantee consistent output to meet requirements; some companies may be aware of this scenario and may choose to mitigate the risk for each situation instead of adjusting the process. What does risk mitigation mean? Risk mitigation has many meanings, depending on variables such as product criticality, customer requirements, or regulations governing the industry. Some common industry risk mitigations are: in-process or final inspections, sorting, testing of each batch, or customer acceptance of cosmetic variation that has no impact on the fit, form, and function of the product. One example of this is variation in the printed circuit board of solder mask (surface coating) color hidden from customer view. Some process parameters that cannot be easily mitigated have more risks and challenges to the company.

Figure 6.2 is a pictorial depiction of a barely capable process.

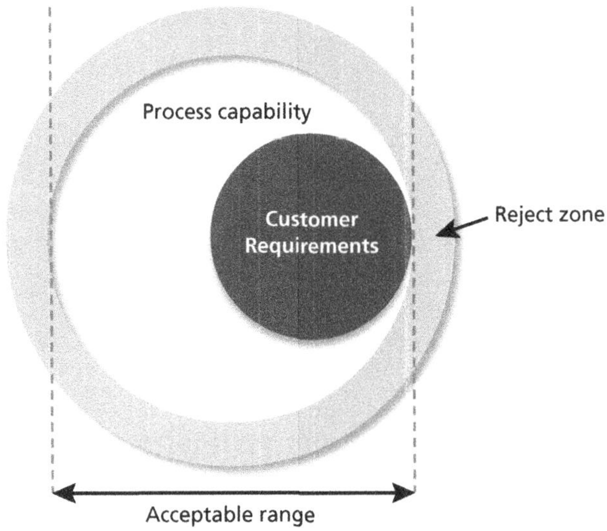

Figure 6.2 Risk and failure mode: process is barely capable; too close to reject zones.

Example 6.2 Barely capable process.

One example is the integrity of a bag sealer. Barely capable process for this example may mean the sealing machine does not have a good sealing integrity and may sometimes leave gaps in the seal. If this machine is for bagging low-cost toys and has no impact on fit, form, function, or safety, it may be more than acceptable to have gaps in the bag seal. For this scenario, the supplier may choose to sort or rework bags with big gaps that will cause the toy inside to fall out during transport. However, if this machine is for creating a sterility barrier for a bag containing a sterilized critical medical device, this fluctuating quality will not be acceptable. The risk involved in failing to identify defective seals for this scenario may cause an expensive litigation, closure of the company, or even injury or death of the patient. With this risk severity, the supplier would likely choose to replace the machine with a capable one or change the process completely to eliminate these risks instead of mitigating the barely capable equipment.

In this failure mode, the process instability and symptoms may be displayed differently, depending on the product or service. Slight variation in the parameters or surrounding environment may push the process to the reject zone if customer requirements are at the edge of the process capability. Products at the edge of the specification may pass final inspections, but may fail during use under certain extreme conditions.

Processes may produce fluctuating metrics that may be perceived as isolated (for example, fluctuating on-time delivery of barely capable logistics plan, fluctuating thickness of copper plating for printed circuit board, fluctuating water purity due to barely capable filtration system).

Lesson Learned:

When inconsistencies such as the examples above are observed, care must be taken so as not to easily dismiss the event as an isolated incident. The signs may be slow, incremental, or sporadic indication of a continuous deterioration. This deterioration may not be easy to recognize because some reviewers may look for a continuous trend before declaring action is needed. Process metrics should not be reviewed as a 'snapshot' of a period, but as an overall process performance measurement.

RISK AND FAILURE MODE: PROCESS IS NOT CAPABLE OR NOT STABLE

In this failure mode, process is not capable and the process parameters are not matching the customer requirements. If the process is left to run 'as is,' it will definitely produce defective or sub-standard output. Normally, one can easily make a decision that this condition is hopeless and change should be done to correct the situation. That is not always the case if you think lean. Before writing off this process into oblivion, one should consider some basic questions.

Why is this process not capable? Is it truly not meeting the output required by the customer? Before changes are implemented, evaluate if there are specific causes for the failure mode giving the perception of non-capable process. One analysis method is the evaluation of the 6Ms.

The 6Ms represent the common elements present in the system:

- Manpower *(e.g., training level, knowledge-base, resource allocation)*
- Machine *(e.g., capability, parameters)*
- Method *(e.g., written procedures to standardize process)*
- Measurement *(e.g., process metrics)*
- Material *(e.g., raw material quality)*
- Mother Nature *(or process environment)*

It is sometimes surprising that a 'non-capable status' may depend on the interpretation of the process parameters. In some cases, it can be compared to the saying *'judgment of beauty (in this case, process capability) is in the eyes of the beholder.'*

Figure 6.3 and the examples that follow show the different perspective of a non-capable process.

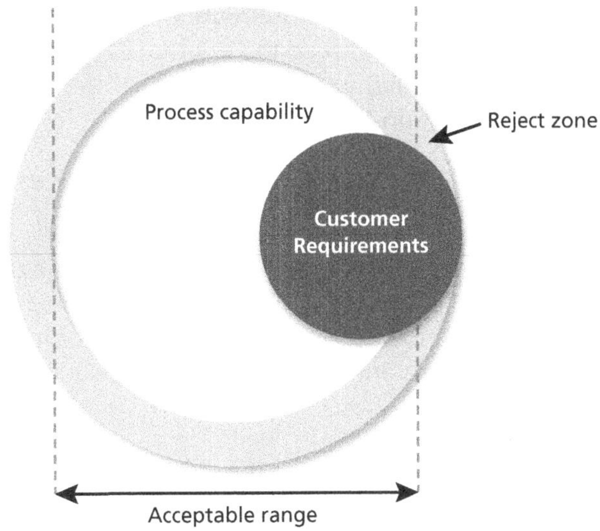

Figure 6.3 Risk and failure mode: process is not capable and/or not stable.

Example 6.3 Stability of a process.

A medical device manufacturing company recently upgraded the clean room to address the control of debris impact on the products. After the installation of expensive clean room certification requirements (e.g., clean room filters, proper air intake/exhaust, etc.), the severity of the debris issue continued to be a problem. After extensive observation of the process, it was discovered that the type of gloves and coats worn by the workers to prevent debris had been recently changed by Purchasing to a lower quality in order to save money. In addition, some of the clean room workers were observed not following clean room coat removal procedures during breaks. These day-to-day non-compliances may have been the culprit of the debris issue, but remained unnoticed until the expensive action plan of upgrading the clean room did not work.

Lesson Learned:

Process variables need in-depth evaluation before changes are implemented. Major changes must have thorough validation, extending to the success factors associated with the change.

RISK AND FAILURE MODE: PROCESS METRICS NOT CALIBRATED FOR INTENDED USE

The alignment of process capability with customer requirements is one of the critical components of a successful metric. But as shown in Fig 6.1, a 'perfect' alignment of the process and customer requirements is not a 100% guarantee that performance goal will be met. Remember, the process elements are subject to variation and could possibly exceed the tolerances allocated for each element if not kept under control. Each element has a dynamic interaction with the process with different levels of impact on the overall results.

Example 6.3a Process metrics: *It is not "one size fits all."*

The process metrics for the inventory accuracy of low-value materials will likely have a wider tolerance than the accuracy metrics for high-value items. Delivery metrics for trucks with multiple customer stops and border crossing may have tighter window time tolerance than local deliveries due to higher delay risks.

Lesson Learned:

It is important that distinctions between the purpose and applications are understood during the development of process metrics; otherwise, the metrics will not be properly aligned with stakeholder interest.

NO PERIODIC REVIEW OF PROCESS METRICS AFTER DEPLOYMENT TO DETECT HIDDEN FACTORIES

Alignment of process metrics with the vision and strategic planning as well as periodic monitoring do not necessarily equate to an effective feedback mechanism to the process. What else could go wrong? The scenario below will show the not-so-visible twist and turn that can make the metrics crumble.

Example 6.4 *"Hidden factories in plain view—Double Dipping."*

A department may purposely or unintentionally double report man-hours as part of productivity. How can this be?

Take, for example, the assembly operators who made incorrect assemblies by installing the wrong parts. Before the units reached the finished assembly inspection station, where the units would have been rejected for rework, the supervisor noticed the discrepancy. The supervisor asked the operator to bring back the wrong assemblies to the beginning of the line instead of forwarding them to the next process (i.e., inspection station). The units were corrected and passed the inspection. These units were not marked 'rework' and therefore not tagged under the rework metric. On the other hand, since productivity is measured by the number of hours and volume processed, it looks like the productivity metric was met as the hidden rework was passed on as part of positive productivity.

Lesson Learned:

There should have been a secondary metric in this scenario (such as 'materials request for replacement parts') to capture the hidden factory (i.e., rework) that occurred in this scenario. Whether the misleading numbers were erroneously presented or whether data were purposely maneuvered to retain the invisibility of the 'hidden factory' remains a question. It is therefore more productive to move forward and re-design the process metrics to get a better picture of the system's performance.

How Does the System Detect and Prevent the Potential Causes of Process Metrics Failure?

PDCA (plan-do-check-act) is one of the common industry practices applicable in the detection and prevention of these failures. The examples presented in this chapter show that failure can occur at any given point regardless of process alignment or misalignment with the requirements. The installation of detection or measurement points is unique to the company's business profile and direction. This book presents the scenarios and tools as lessons learned to be applied in the manner applicable to the business and process owner's objectives.

7

Moment of Truth: Another Expression of Risks, Possible Failure Mode, and Process Metric

The phrase *moment of truth* has many meanings, depending on the situation. In a nutshell, a customer's moment of truth is a deciding moment that can mean winning or losing a business bid based on that decisive moment. It may be something as simple as a warm greeting to a visiting customer that gives the impression of a responsive service provider or a clean and well maintained parking lot that gives the impression of a quality company. Sometimes it's things like this that seal the business partnership.

"The customer's perception, if it lingers long enough, may become the customer's reality." It is therefore beneficial to maintain consistent and positive moments of truth as part of the business philosophy.

As shown in Figure 7.1, a moment of truth is a brief perception that may swing the balance that holds the fate of a business growth or failure.

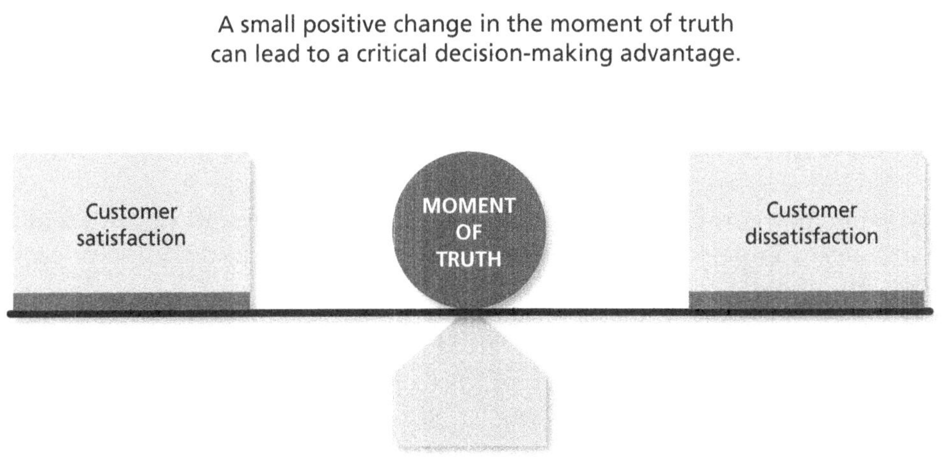

Figure 7.1 Pictorial representation of a moment of truth.

When you call for a service, whether for a pizza delivery or dishwasher repair, the first encounter you have with the service provider is the voice that answers your call. The voice gives you that first impression on the type of service you expect to receive. When you call a Customer Service department to complain about receiving the wrong product, after it was lost for a week, the first voice that greets you sometimes determines the level of frustration you plan to unload on that first unlucky voice that answers the call queue. When a potential customer visits a plant for a qualification audit, the overall cleanliness of the facility or the friendliness of the receptionist may play a part in winning or losing the business bid. Some quality professionals call these first impressions 'moments of truth.' These are the brief but precious moments of encounter with a customer or stakeholder that will give an impression that may have a tremendous impact on the long-term business relationship. These moments of truth may last within those moments or may last for a lifetime. Encounters that last for a lifetime are the positive moments of truth.

An irate customer greeted coldly by the telephone operator may become more hostile due to increased frustration with the company. The operator represents the product provider that caused the customer's dissatisfaction and being treated in this cold fashion 'adds salt to the injury.' In this particular case, the customer may have been expecting a reassuring and knowledgeable voice to listen to the problem and offer a resolution. These are the customer's moments of truth—these happen every day, many times a day. Are these moments of truth important to the business or should these be dismissed as 'a routine part of the job'?

The moments of truth may sound trivial and of no quantifiable added value. In fact, moments of truth may be one of the critical keys to a business success. Moments of truth are spontaneous, unrehearsed, and give the customers a peek preview of the company's values, philosophy, commitment to customer satisfaction, and ethics—important elements in long-term business partnership.

Can these moments of truth be part of performance metrics and feedback to the system? Absolutely! But how?

There are many ways to capture and quantify these moments of truth that may have significant impact on business partners' relationship and company growth. Some examples are:

- Sending a brief customer survey after completing a service.
- Counting the frequency of request for a certain repair person.
- Randomly monitoring customer complaint calls as part of the procedure (to assess quality of responses to the customer).
- Tracking frequency of repeat shoppers visiting a store location other than the one nearest their residence selling the same products (e.g., credit card or store card traces residency).

- Trending of customer comments after each encounter (e.g., during sales meeting, plant visits, telephone call, etc.). These impromptu customer comments may be accumulated as part of the customer survey. The challenge faced by most companies is the breakdown of this element to reveal the inner layer not easily visible or detectable by traditional customer focus initiatives.

Moments of truth are candid moments revealing how the workforce interacts with the internal or external customers and stakeholders. This is the test of the company's core values, unrehearsed. Each day, simple moments of truth can cumulatively make a big impact on some business elements that management may not even notice until the negative event reaches a no-tolerance zone.

It is even more critical to maintain a positive moment of truth in a high-risk or precarious situations wherein a hairline change may mean success or failure. An example is a potential minor issue that escalated into a major non-conformance based on the manager's 'lack of concern' response to the ISO auditor. This response sealed the auditor's perception that there was no commitment to the requirements. Visual depiction of the moment of truth scenario is shown in Figure 7.2.

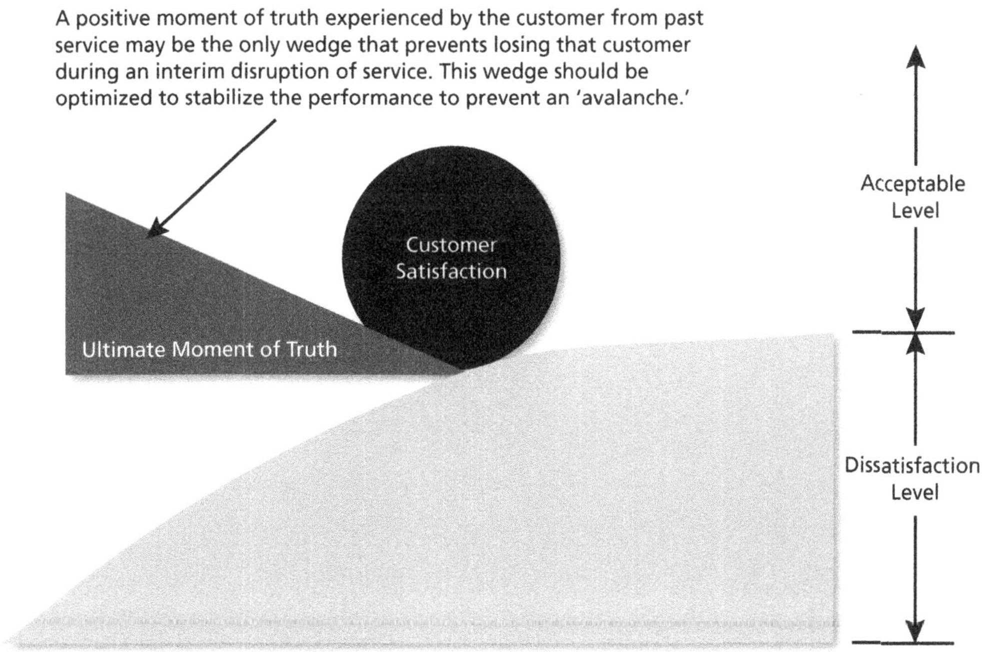

Figure 7.2 Ultimate moment of truth.

Reference: "Mitigation During Moment of Truth" authored by Janet Smith and published in *Audit Division Newsletter*, June 2015.

Example 7.1 Customer's perspective: moment of truth.

The front desk receptionist puts a customer call on hold for a few minutes to answer walk-in people. This may have been assumed acceptable since no one has formally complained about it. The person at the other end of the line was the CEO of a potential business partner wanting to have lunch with the Operations Manager to finalize his business partnership proposal. After a few minutes on hold, the CEO made his decision, that this company is not fit to be his business partner. He would not want his customers to be put hold that long giving the perception that the customer call was not important.

Lesson Learned:

The company should provide a procedure and training on how to handle and prioritize calls and walk-in inquiries to ensure customers are provided the expected service in a timely manner. As applicable, a priority list of expected calls should be given to the receptionist. Peak periods should be identified so as to have a contingency plan in place, such as a back-up person to answer inquiries. The tone of voice and demeanor of the receptionist plays a significant role in encouraging the customer to have patience while waiting in queue. These are simple, inexpensive techniques that could have secured that potential business partnership.

8

Process Metrics: Measurement of Risk and Failure Modes

Measurement of any change or improvement should be monitored through the selection of metrics directly or closely associated with the element being measured. This chapter shows examples of different risks and failure modes when the processes metrics or quality criteria are not fulfilled to meet stakeholder expectations. In some cases, one has to be creative in developing indirect metrics to measure the mitigation of a risk or impact of a failure event. Think of process metrics in terms of the buoyancy concept. In cases where the risk or failure mode is not easily visible for measurement, it is sometimes easier to measure its impact (see Figure 8.1). It is not unusual to adjust the initiatives if the opposing forces are gaining momentum.

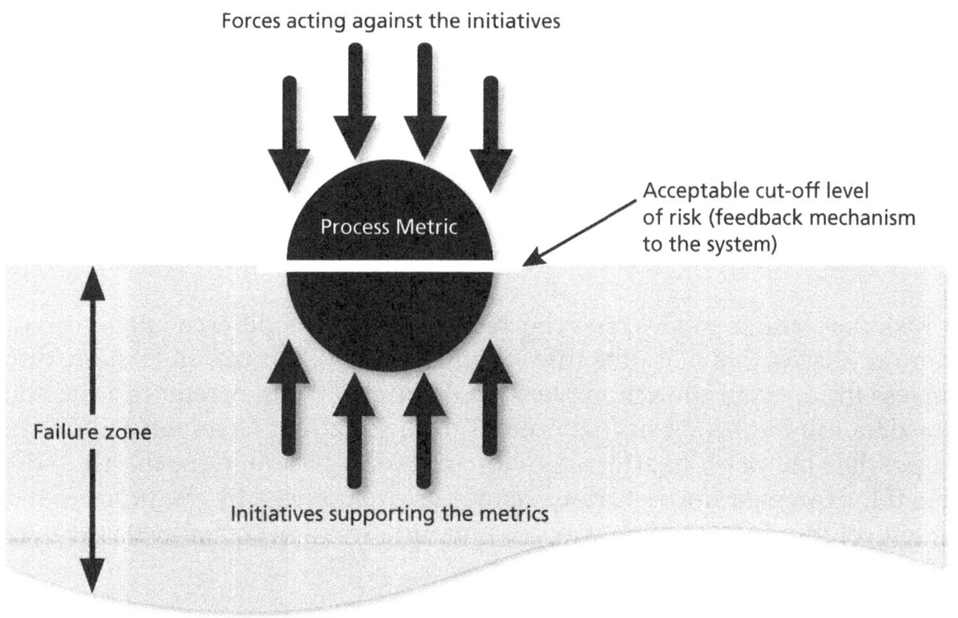

Figure 8.1 Process metrics: measurement of initiative effectiveness.

In simple translation, the negative forces acting against the goal (e.g., waste, errors, silos, etc.) must be counteracted by the initiatives to keep the process metrics 'afloat.' In this buoyancy comparison, the density of these negative forces may submerge the initiative completely, making it more difficult to salvage. The solution is to keep monitoring (through audit or structured performance review) the 'submersion level' of this buoyancy system by recognizing the signs and early detection indicators. Early indication of deviations from the acceptable submersion level (i.e., process metric) should alert and prepare the system for a root cause analysis. This early warning will help identify, contain, and mitigate the opposing forces to prevent further acceleration that could lead to a point beyond control.

Example 8.1 Visible surface may not show the true risk or failure core.

Repeating assembly errors were attributed to customer's complex specification; after an in-depth root cause analysis it was concluded that training was not effective due to the non-standard relay of information to the new hires. Part of the action taken was the reinforcement of a more effective training of new employees to minimize expensive errors or scrap, etc. In this example, the additional metric would be the measurement of the training effectiveness of new hires to reduce the error rate metric. Examples: Error rate, cycle time to complete a job versus the standard time, productivity, etc.

Lesson Learned:

Precaution must be taken when reacting to potential risks or failure modes, as the visible surface may not necessarily show the severity of the risk or the failure mode. Potential risk or failure mode is sometimes misleading; therefore, it is important to interpret the indicators that may help uncover the failure root cause and severity of risk for proper resolution.

Risks or failure modes may be hidden behind a different name or under common 'aliases' that mask the true identity (root causes), making it more difficult to assess the appropriate action plans. In some cases, it may require a drill-down, deep data mining to get to the 'bottom' of a situation. Common failure modes and possible metrics for early mitigation of risks are listed in the matrix shown in Table 8.1, expressed under various names as experienced by the process owners. The left column lists possible ways of quantifying these sometimes vague failure mode descriptions.

Table 8.1 Process metrics, risks, and failure modes.

Risks or failure modes as indicators of poor performance	Possible process metrics to detect and measure severity of failures
Poor productivity	• Cycle time • Acceptable quality output quantity (not just a volume measurement)
Lack of training	• Validation of knowledge effectiveness via test score • Error rate
Inefficiency	• Measurement of wastes (such as excessive transportation, inventory, material handling, waiting time, over-processing, error rate)
Roadblocks	• Wait time *Roadblocks, at times, may be abstract in the eyes of the workers as they may come from different directions. However, one universal measurement is time wasted waiting to get a task done. The waiting may be for paperwork coming from the customer before a product can be released for shipment or for the stockroom to find the needed parts.*
Poor resource planning	• Overtime hours • Ratio of output versus workforce
Ineffective contract review	• Price quote versus actual quote after learning curve (e.g., three months after project kick off)
Defective raw material	• Acceptance or rejection rate of the raw material
Machine not working	• Downtime • Frequency of changeover • Frequency of unplanned preventive maintenance
Sub-optimization of manpower	• Accomplishment rate of expected projects or tasks for the job description or time management *Example: Use of a manager's time to perform a receiving clerk job to meet demand due to poor resource allocation is a sub-optimization of a managerial salary and time.*
Sub-standard product	• Reject rate
Low morale	• Absenteeism • Error rate

(continued)

Table 8.1 Process metrics, risks, and failure modes. *(continued)*

Risks or failure modes as indicators of poor performance	Possible process metrics to detect failure modes
Poor safety	• Accident rate
Environmental condition	• Emission rate • Regulatory report rate
Poor housekeeping	• Product contamination level • Errors due to mix up • Damages of products due to improper storage
Inaccurate inventory	• Availability rate • Lead time/trend of material release to production (is release cycle time within the acceptable window time?)
Unhappy customer	• Number of complaints versus product shipped • Number of claims or returns • Lost accounts
Lack of accountability	• Error rate (repeating error may be due to lack of ownership)
Hidden defective units	• Frequency of request for replacement parts *This may be a hidden factory if defective units are produced and not logged as rejects but 'put aside' for rework; other indicators of rework may be used to track this hidden factory, such as requests for replacement parts.* **Example 8.1a** Obsolescence rate of materials In certain cases wherein a defective product cannot be reworked, it may be 'quarantined' in the hidden factory until it reaches obsolescence. An example is the quarantining of pastry dough manufactured with the wrong ingredients. Operations may put the 'wrong product' in the freezer while investigating root cause of error until the shelf life of the material runs out. Then it is problem solved (i.e., hidden). Material is disposed of as obsolete rather than rejected.

(continued)

Table 8.1 Process metrics, risks, and failure modes. *(continued)*

Risks or failure modes as indicators of poor performance	Possible process metrics to detect failure modes
Errors due to lack of attention to details	• Performance metrics (output versus error rate) *Some workers may have higher accuracy level than others performing the same tasks due to some variables not easily visible to the system.*
	Example 8.2 For example, a super performer may have zero defects because this person works during the first shift with full preventive maintenance support when the machine breaks down. The poor guy working on the off shift has no support and has to perform machine troubleshooting in addition to running the machine, which leads to more errors than the first shift. **Lesson Learned:** Performance metric has many faces and should be evaluated carefully before reaching a conclusion.
Operator's poor prioritization of tasks causing late deliveries	• Time study to measure cycle time allotted to perform task versus actual time needed to perform tasks *Poor resource allocation may be the real issue if the manager did not have the accurate standard cycle time for tasks versus resources needed.*
	• Change request rate outside window time *Another feasible culprit could be the customer's freedom to change the order after it has been released for manufacturing. There should be a change cut-off time. If the company allows changes beyond the cut-off time, there should be some contingency plan to ensure meeting both the customer and operational requirements.*
Poor communication with customer	• Delay (in hours or days) before company notifies customer of a delayed shipment. • Number of follow up inquiries before the customer receives the information. • Compliance to established timeline to respond to customer complaints (Example, containment to be sent within 24 hours, root cause analysis to be sent within 48 hours, etc.)

9

The Many Faces of Ineffective Process Metrics

One may think that the perfect metrics have been designed as the gatekeeper of improvement initiatives. All the critical detection points are covered for early warning of possible deviation so timely mitigation may be applied just like a first aid kit. When you think you have covered the practical aspects of the process metric system, you come to realize, maybe through routine walk of the operations floor or review of records pertaining to a customer complaint, that there are many faces of the process metrics. The many faces are hidden from view and the system sometimes sees only the 'good side' while the 'dark side' is buried in a hidden factory eating away profit, customer satisfaction, internal growth, and other opportunities.

While the system is focused on the good side, the dark side is slowly weakening the roots of stability until the system collapses. The system may be oblivious of the hidden factory; however, in some cases, it may be known to a select few. The select few may tolerate or even cultivate the hidden factory either by choice for personal gain or due to inability to manage it.

What are these many faces of ineffective process metrics? How do you recognize them so they can be avoided? Each face changes with the situation, so there is no universal answer in the recognition and avoidance of each face. Logical application of the sample tools discussed in this book should help to increase the knowledge bandwidth and minimize this chameleon's chance of existence. Here are some examples.

THE MANY FACES OF INEFFECTIVE PROCESS METRICS (ALSO KNOWN AS RISKS OR FAILURE MODE)

Operational Activities 'Outrunning' Quality Results to Error

Operational process metrics reflecting the operation's success are the most visible in the eyes of the stakeholders (Figure 9.1). Productivity may be a leading process metric, but if it outruns quality, then gaps such as error rate and other failures may occur.

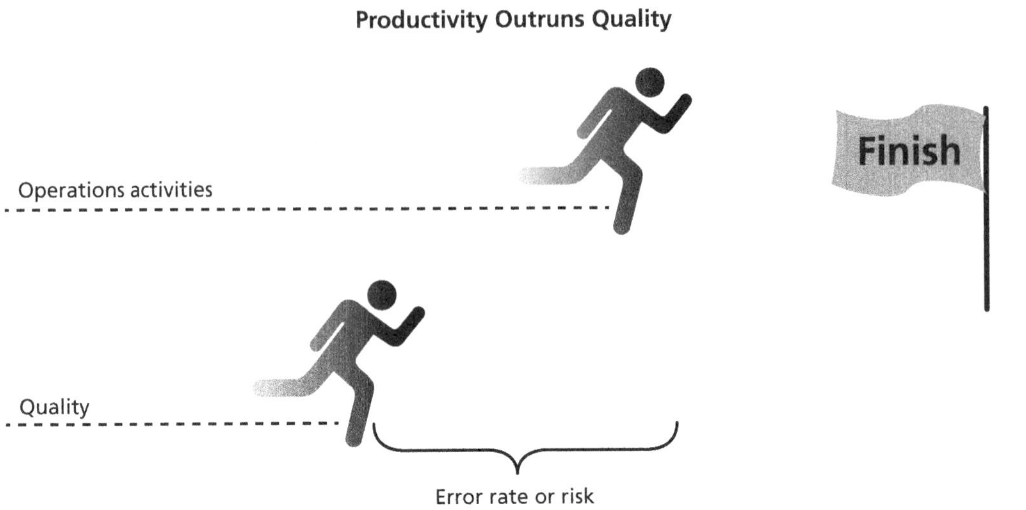

Figure 9.1 One source of error rate and sub-optimization.

Reference: "Do not be Mislead by Productivity Measures" published by ASQ *Quality Progress* magazine, August 2012, Janet Bautista Smith.

Example 9.1 Productivity must not outrun quality.

The CEO may praise Operations for the volume processed for the quarter, but beneath this volume may be defects not yet uncovered for the period. This gap will probably be uncovered in incremental proportions as the defects reach the end users.

Lesson Learned:

Countermeasure metrics should be considered to help ensure a balanced measurement program. It will also help prevent silos and promote neutrality and integrity of the metrics.

Example 9.2 Do numbers lie?

Another example is the promotion of the Operations Manager for keeping the resource number the same and meeting the volume demands of new accounts. Not all internal errors can be immediately detected prior to shipping the products; thus, in this example, the error rate resulting from shortcuts to beat the process cycle time may not be visible until the products reach the end users.

Lesson Learned:

Process streamlining through continuous improvement and waste reduction will have a significant positive impact on process cycle without jeopardizing quality. This should be the first option rather than taking shortcuts to 'beat the cycle time.'

How can this be prevented? One way is through the implementation of a secondary metric, as applicable, or layered metrics to counterbalance the primary metric (e.g., productivity versus error rate). Biased metrics may be deliberate or unintentional; whatever the case may be, there are precautions that can be devised within the metric system to minimize or prevent such situations in a quantified manner.

CAN 1% METRIC RULE?

"It is the best performance we can achieve; 99% is excellent; customer should be happy with this metric." Sounds familiar? Sadly, this is not an uncommon response coming from some sectors of the supply chain.

So can the one percent metric rule? Yes—if that one percent is a critical element to the stakeholders. In the diagram shown (Figure 9.2), the one percent failure may be acceptable to the supplier; but if that one percent caused a plant shutdown or major product recall for the customer, then that one percent rules. The impact of that one percent failure should be the deciding point whether that one percent is an acceptable part of the inherent process noise or it needs further root cause analysis. Stakeholders input (e.g., customer, internal process) is critical in assessing the process capability and the feasibility of meeting the requirements.

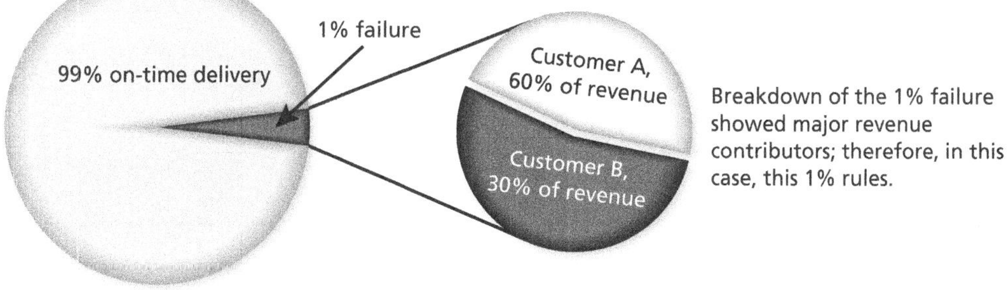

Figure 9.2 Can one percent metric rule?

Reference: "Can One Percent Rule?" published by ASQ *Lean Division* Newsletter, August 2013, Janet Bautista Smith.

PERFORMANCE METRICS WITHOUT SUSTAINABILITY

Have you heard of people getting promoted because of a one-time project that made a big 'splash' or instant glory that captured the system's attention? The splash may have had no potential for sustainability but it was eagerly accepted by the system. How can this happen? It may have been accepted because of a deteriorating system hungry for change in a company willing to take a risk, when decisions may have been based on a short-sighted vision, or when biased bosses were blinded by this short-lived splash that looked shiny and rich with potential value to the system. Before it can be proven as a short-lived initiative, the initiator hands it off to the process owners and tries to start another 'splash' somewhere. The poor process owners left with the 'hot potato' take the blame for not maintaining the initiative and letting it collapse to failure (Figure 9.3).

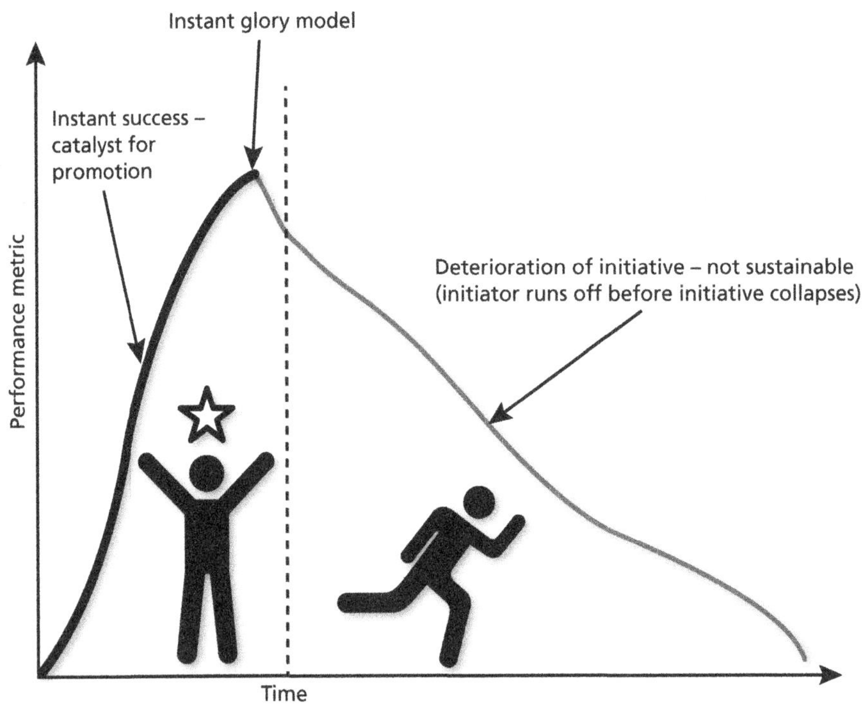

Figure 9.3 Process metrics without sustainability.

Reference: *Concept from Auditing Beyond Compliance,* Quality Press, 2012, Janet Bautista Smith.

How can this be prevented? Improvement projects should have a validation period to prove effectiveness through process metrics measured against a benchmark and company goal. The validation period does not have to be complicated; it can be a simple gap analysis audit identifying current status or measurement of the process being affected versus the desired state or the expected improvement metric. Without this comparison, it is difficult to judge whether the initiative is really an added value that needs maintenance or is just a short-lived continuous improvement 'look-alike.' If it is not an added-value, the company will not only suffer loss of resources or time but may also suffer from missed opportunities. The improvement 'look-alike' may have depleted and wasted the available resources and may also have misguided and diverted other initiatives to failure.

There is no one simple answer to prevent this fiasco, although process metrics installed in the right position may help detect and prevent this situation. However, a metric's signal to the system will not be effective if the signal is ignored. Signals need to be recognized and evaluated and, as applicable, should trigger action plans.

Creation of a hand-off policy or procedure listing the required milestones for the hand-off will help reduce the probability of similar occurrence in the future. The hand-off may require, for example, a validation period to observe results prior to official transfer to the process owners.

PROCESS METRIC: TWO FACES

The concept of laminate flooring is a good analogy of a process metric with two surfaces. Just like the laminate flooring example, a metric may have an underlayment that can hide the defects or negative variance as the byproduct of the positive metric.

An example of this concept is the on-time delivery process metric. Operations may have poorly quoted manufacturing a product line that exceeded the available capability or capacity; adjustment of the customer-accepted quote was not an option. Therefore, the possible alternative to cope with the customer requirements using the existing resources may have been the overtime option or shortcuts that would eventually cause errors. Just like the laminate material shown in Figure 9.4, the bumps or imperfections buried in the hidden factory will eventually cause deterioration if the performance metrics' design continues to hide these non-conformances. The subfloor represents the process or system and the subfloor defects represent variables, not easily visible but with negative impact on the performance level and stability of the system.

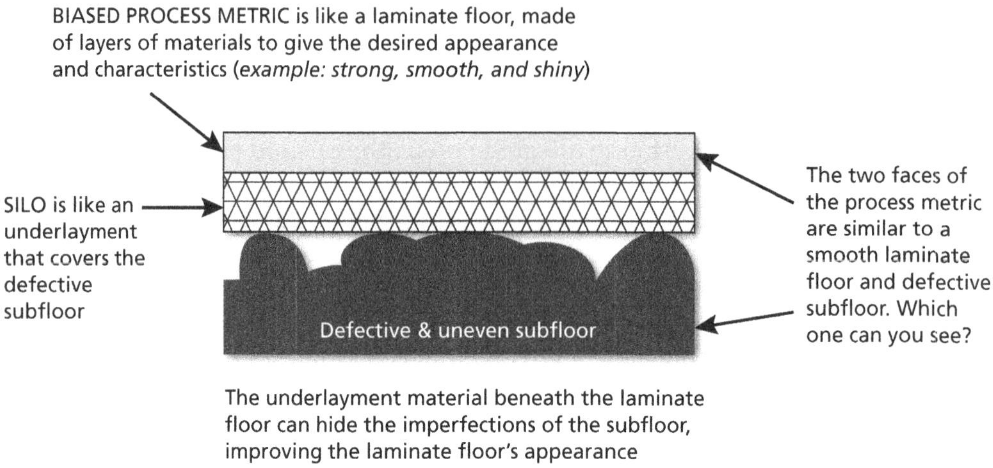

Figure 9.4 Two-faced process metric.

Some examples of these hidden variables are sub optimization of talent, such as underutilization of capable personnel due to inexperienced management or internal silos.

Example 9.3 The hidden factory.

A new manager may micro-manage certain talents in fear of being outshined, thus curbing the creativity and growth of the talent. A manager might use another's talent to hide incompetency in the position (for example, consistently using a team approach to solicit ideas from unsuspecting team-spirited members and then discreetly claiming ownership and implementing these stolen ideas stripped of identity).

Lesson Learned:

How to prevent silos and promote a work ethic? There are many programs to address these questions, such as promotion of fairness and the reward of desired behavior. Reward is not necessarily in monetary terms; reward may be recognition and appreciation of efforts and contribution of people 'working behind the scene.' It takes good leadership to recognize these shadows working behind the stage curtain to provide support to the leading character on the stage. These are the vital grassroots level workers who may not necessarily take the center stage and yet may be carrying the majority of the hands-on workload to support the initiative.

Below are some examples of how hidden factories are started and the mitigation methods to keep the system healthy:

- **Reckless decision making** may result in failure 'hidden under the rug' and slowly dissipated into the system to further hide identification. Sound decision making should include measurable deliverables.
- **Miscalculation of risks and consequences** based on faulty information. The installation of a monitoring system (audit program) and versatile, layered performance metrics would curtail these hidden factories.
- **Intentional diversion of initiatives** for personal gain, without consideration of impact on the overall system, will eventually cause the collapse of the program. Cross-checks and balances should be part of the initiatives as countermeasures against potential bias.

Misaligned Expectations

Some metrics may not be satisfactory, not because of poor process output but because of misaligned expectations (see Figure 9.5). It can be compared with the expectation that an ordinary tree can grow into a giant Sequoia. This type of expectation is not only unrealistic, but impossible.

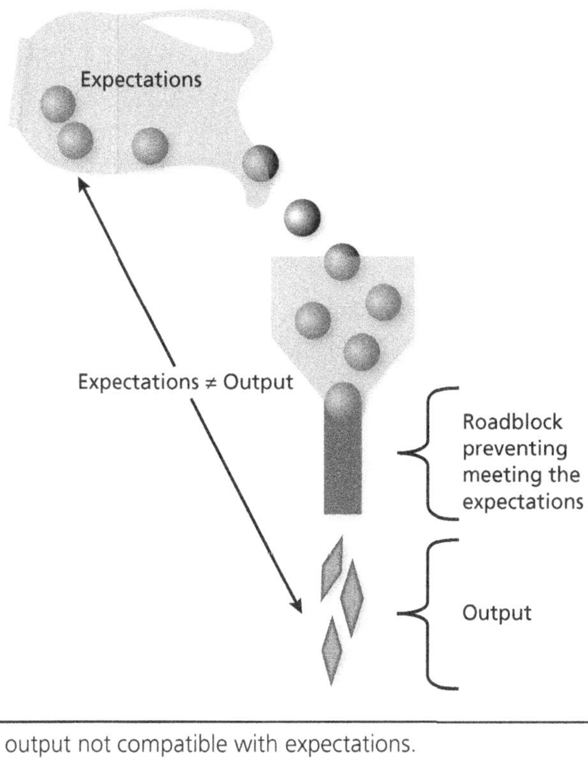

Figure 9.5 Initiative output not compatible with expectations.

Some Initiatives Take Longer to Mature

Some expectations may not consider the practical timeline involved with the desired results; some initiatives may take longer to take root in the system, some initiatives may give incremental results rather than a one-time big growth spurt. The acceleration of the initiative's maturity is dependent on the dynamics of its reaction to its environment; some initiatives, just like plant growth, may be achieved through the introduction of plant hormones or catalyst. The catalyst may trigger an outburst of change or growth, but may not necessarily sustain the expected level of development.

Initiative's Capability is Limited

In some cases, achievement of the initiative's peak potential may not necessarily guarantee the stakeholder's ultimate satisfaction. Why? The initiative's capability does not match the goal. The goal may have been set higher than the selected initiative's capability to produce the expected output. This limitation may be in the form of manpower, method, or technology optimized to the maximum limit and yet fail to yield the expected level performance.

Example 9.4 Identification of process capability versus requirements.

A manager assigned to optimize savings through the streamlining of manpower and process with minimum error faces a challenge with high failure risk if not supported by the organization. The challenge is compounded if the situation involves roadblocks, for example dependence on manual detection of errors. In this case, the streamlining of manpower and the achievement of minimizing the process errors may be difficult unless other options are considered (e.g., change in technology to allow automation or simplified process to minimize human intervention).

This scenario is headed towards disaster if not properly mitigated at an early stage.

Lesson Learned:

Roadblocks should be identified, documented, and escalated so they do not become part of a hidden factory. A simple process flowchart showing the core processes may be applicable to identify the possible roadblocks or bottlenecks. A time study of the core steps including the supporting activities (e.g., waiting time, hand-off from one process, paperwork) will provide more accuracy in the assessment of the process cycle. The process cycle time compared with the available man hours to support the volume demand will help the manager increase the visibility of the resource allocation need for management support.

PROCESS METRIC EXPECTATION IS MISUNDERSTOOD; A MOVING TARGET?

Failure to meet the expected result may be due to the misunderstanding of management's direction. Clarity of the vision and strategy is of utmost importance so these elements may be drilled down successfully to the grassroots level through day-to-day activities. This can be easily addressed through a communication system within the company that includes the grassroots level's participation and input. Some companies tend to consider 'communication' as the regular meetings happening in the board room where formal presentations of plans or financial reports are discussed amongst the select circle of management. Information from these important meetings serves as the guidance to the workforce if deployed effectively. However, if not communicated to the grassroots level, basic information impacting day-to-day activities may not be necessarily aligned with this guiding principle. Management's expectations translated into day-to-day operations reinforce the grassroots workers' embrace of the expected culture and behavior to support the company vision and strategy. Without understanding these fundamental elements, it is impossible to synchronize the individual grassroots efforts into a unified driver of improvement. It is like the football game. The coach or quarterback pulls the team together to ensure understanding of the strategies for each move (initiative) to increase the possibility of meeting the touchdown objective for each major maneuver. If the receiver (grassroots worker) is not cognizant of the maneuver (i.e., strategy), competition will get the ball. It is that simple.

10

Leverage Measureable Results; Act on Process Indicators!

The measurements of success discussed in previous chapters give another insight on the role of root cause analysis as an improvement tool and savings generator. The root cause analysis of gaps for improvement initiatives will increase the visibility of this initiative's added value and help capture stakeholder interest in prioritizing this program. This is one of the critical steps. Once you have stakeholder attention, the expectation to show positive changes and measurable results will be the next focal point. The improvement initiatives are like the starter seeds for a garden. These seeds need nurturing to grow into optimum maturity for harvesting. The starter seeds are like the statistical analysis reports, which mean nothing to the stakeholders if not cultivated into actionable items to enrich the system. Statistical trends and creative reports are passive information without added value unless put into action.

Sometimes, it is challenging to start the 'ball rolling' to get the maximum leverage on these measured performance metrics; thus, it is not uncommon that these statistical analyses and reports remain as mere decorations on the bulletin boards after hours of collection and documentation. In some cases, these reports are updated and reported but no actions are taken to truly measure the improvement variance. Why? There are many reasons.

- Wrong seeds are being cultivated (i.e., wrong metric selection, therefore wrong indicator).
- Unnecessary information (i.e., process noise) creates confusion in the system and can mislead the prioritization process (i.e., inability to choose the vital few).

Example 10.1 Too much information, no action.

A manager created several metrics as a gauge of the department's process control. Due to the number of variables being measured, the manager checked the status of metrics below the goal by verbally asking the assigned operator about the root cause and the action plan to address the issue during the daily shift meetings. However, there was no time to verify each root cause due to the sheer volume of the metrics being discussed during the review period.

Lesson Learned:

Focus should be on the *vital few* instead of tackling too many metrics superficially. More time would be available to perform a more in-depth root cause and trend analysis of the critical metrics if resources were not "spread too thin" measuring numerous metrics. Verbal verification without in-depth analysis is a waste of time as the method is superficial and not based on substantial fact-finding. It also sends the wrong message to the process owners. *"If management does not care to verify the true root cause, why should I?"*

- No accountability *(i.e., process owners should be involved in the action plans, so there is more vested interest).*

Example 10.2 Counterbalancing of metrics.

The Manufacturing manager is responsible for the activities performed in the center including resource allocation, productivity, and on-time delivery. These metrics are being met at the cost of quality when volume peaks up since the time constraint pushes the workers to prioritize on-time delivery as the leading metric. As volume goes up, the error rate is predicted to go up but not seen until later. The Quality department, on the other hand, is responsible for ensuring compliance and error prevention. During departmental performance reviews, the Operations manager has the center stage and the Quality department stays at the back stage. Expectations to prevent the errors failed as reflected in the number of complaints and returns.

Lesson Learned:

Metrics reflecting accountability on error prevention should be included in the operational metrics (for example, scrap rate per shipment). Reasons for the scrap should be analyzed and trended to identify sources of errors so efforts can be focused in the prevention. It will also serve as countermeasure of the favored metrics and the consideration of the 'side effects' of the primary metrics (in this case, productivity and on-time delivery).

- Lack of employee motivation and acknowledgement *(embrace of the culture must be from within).*
- Silo within the organization prevents free flow of information *(information blockage creates roadblocks).*

Example 10.3 Silos (hidden from view).

Some customers do not necessarily file a formal complaint when minor deviations are noted in the product. Instead, the customer notifies the customer representative so the information can be relayed back to the system to prevent recurrence in next shipments. The customer representatives report the information to Operations, but the usual answer is: "those are minor cosmetic imperfection, not affecting anything." The frustrated customer representative continues to receive this information from the customer but keeps the information in a silo to avoid confrontation with Operations. This situation continues until the discrepancy can no longer be tolerated and the customer switches to another manufacturer that can fulfill the requirements.

Lesson Learned:

The customer's incremental dissatisfaction, although reported, was not addressed due to an internal silo. A written customer feedback system should be created to provide a communication tool that can be used instead of verbal communication that turns into a confrontation. There has to be a metric to capture the voice of the customer for early mitigation or root cause analysis of possible trend.

- Metric that cannot be changed, so why choose this metric?

Example 10.4 Prioritize what to measure.

A diminishing product line is kept active to benefit from the small but steady demand until its end of cycle. Gathering capability information (process metrics) for this line will not be beneficial as it is not cost effective to perform any adjustment at this phase.

Lesson Learned:

If you cannot change or improve the metric, do not measure it! It is a waste of time; measure something else. It is not uncommon to find that the process owners gathering the metrics are unaware of the strategy in place as shown in this example. One way to prevent this waste is to increase visibility of metrics to appropriate teams (e.g., displayed on bulletin boards or announced weekly via email). If metrics are not shared for review, then it is an expensive way of utilizing record keepers.

So, how can we leverage these measurable results? *Acting on these results is the simple answer!* Identification of roadblocks to address issues is a team effort! Collecting data and doing nothing about it is not only wasteful but also a bad example of non-commitment to resolving issues to promote improvement. The process metrics, if used properly, are the indicators that would help the company get closer to the achievement of goals.

PART III
Root Causes

11

Root Cause Analysis Life Cycle

DEFINING THE PROBLEM

Root cause analysis is not an easy task. It takes an open and creative mind to uncover possible situations that may have contributed to the incident under investigation. Before this can happen, some mind bending tasks may occur. The crucial elements associated with the problem statement must be data mined and made visible at the start of the root cause analysis process. Failure to do this integral part of the process may cause a blockage in unraveling the true root cause and the formulation of an effective corrective action plan. In some cases, pressure and time constraints to meet deadlines may lead to incomplete or inaccurate problem statements lacking the critical-to-quality elements to attain an effective analysis and resolution. In some situations, it is not unusual to unknowingly accept a poor root cause analysis as a trade-off for time with the intent to re-visit the issue later. This paradigm is flawed; it may be more costly and risky, if this situation occurs as the norm rather than extreme exception. The erroneous problem will lead to a wrong analysis, and therefore ineffective resolution. One might ask, how can this be prevented?

There are several paths to prevent this potential disaster. The concept chosen for this publication is the DMAIC methodology (define-measure-analyze-improve-control, also in Chapter 2), combined with other lean tools in this chapter. This model provides a guideline in the development, deployment, and sustainability of an effective lean-based root cause analysis program. This will also provide measurable results and savings on any associated improvement opportunities identified in the evaluation.

Figure 11.1 depicts the root cause analysis flow integrated with the lean concept. This simple model explains the cultural mindset that will facilitate the breakthrough in using the old concept (i.e., root cause analysis) partnered with lean tools to rejuvenate the added value benefits.

This flow will become clearer with the actual examples demonstrating practical implementation and measurable resolutions discussed in the following chapters.

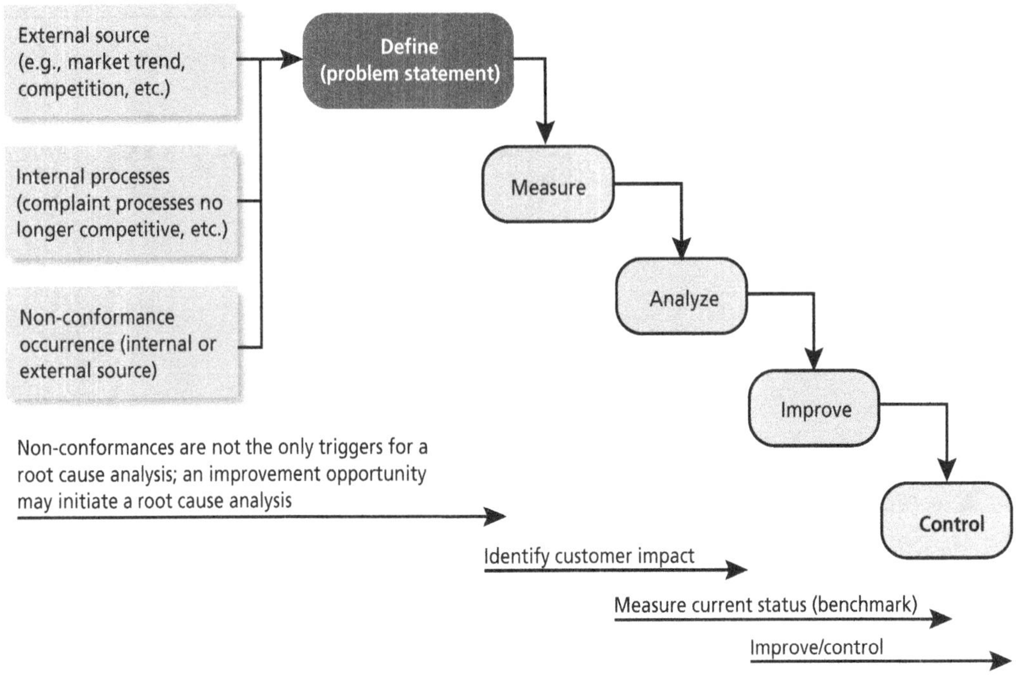

Figure 11.1 Lean dynamic root cause analysis model.

The DMAIC model provides a structured guideline in defining the very first step in root cause analysis, the problem statement, as well as the other elements of the root cause analysis as shown in Figure 11.1. The common mistakes in this first step are the lack of visibility and recognition of the different layers encompassing 'problem statement.' Problem statement is like an onion with several layers protecting the core. It is not uncommon to leave an onion in the refrigerator for months before suddenly remembering that you need it for a menu item. Is it still edible or rotten inside? (The layers may be blocking the rotten portion.) Cutting the onion into halves easily exposes all the layers and a decision can be made once these layers are exposed. This simple analogy explains the lean-based problem statement. There are many layers to consider and assessment can only be made if these layers are visible or measurable. Do we have to look at every single minute layer for detailed inspection? Absolutely not! That approach would not be considered lean. The lean approach is to select the vital few that will have significant impact on the expected results. The concept of the vital few, also known as Pareto analysis, helps screen the influx of information, allowing users to focus mainly on the critical problems that are likely to have significant impact on the issue of interest (see Figure 11.2). Otherwise, with limited resources and time constraints, it will create a roadblock if all the variables are treated with the same priority or severity.

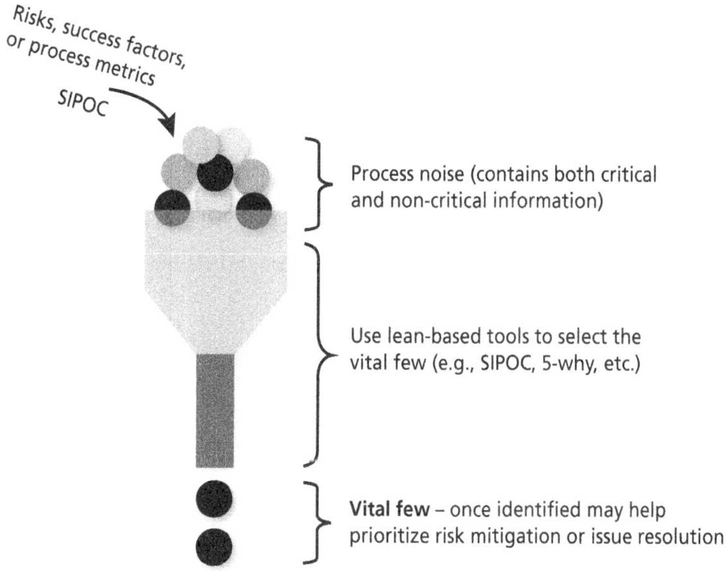

Figure 11.2 Selection of the vital few (also known as Pareto analysis).

The lean approach must also consider the different aspects of the business sustainability and growth during the root cause analysis— financial impact, effect on the internal processes, effect on the workforce, and impact on the internal processes. This methodology is also known as the 'balanced scorecard' approach. As the phrase implies, this strategy has cross checks and balances to help ensure the prevention of biased interest that may result in the system's sub optimization or catastrophic failure. The balanced scorecard approach has a company-wide span that is most beneficial especially when performing root cause analysis of system gaps. Root cause analysis specific to an event or occurrence may benefit more from other lean tools described in this book.

A close analogy is like a chess game wherein the loss of a *pawn* to obtain a piece of greater value is a good move, but the loss of a *queen* due to a hasty decision making may likely lead to failure. The message from this analogy: Identifying the significant layers of the problem and selecting the vital few to start the root cause analysis is a good business approach in considering the critical elements involved. This is also known as risk evaluation.

Weighing the risks or costs associated with the problem layers will narrow down the selection analysis path to develop the optimal resolution design. It is not uncommon to re-define or re-adjust the problem statement based on the information uncovered during the data collection. This is like 'fine tuning' the sight scope to increase the probability of a better aim in hitting the goal. Not knowing the severity and scope of the problem because of a hasty superficial root cause analysis may likely worsen the problem and increase customer dissatisfaction.

A structured and independent root cause analysis will provide a good starting point for the identification of the true problem. Effective root cause analysis will not only enhance the sustainability of the system through the continued feedback on improvement opportunity, but will also serve as a cost savings tool. Most operational problems identified in the root cause analysis have associated variables, such as risk, as depicted in Figure 11.3—this is an opportunity for improvement and savings! The improvement and savings do not have to be monumental. They could be incremental in value but with huge cumulative effect in the long run.

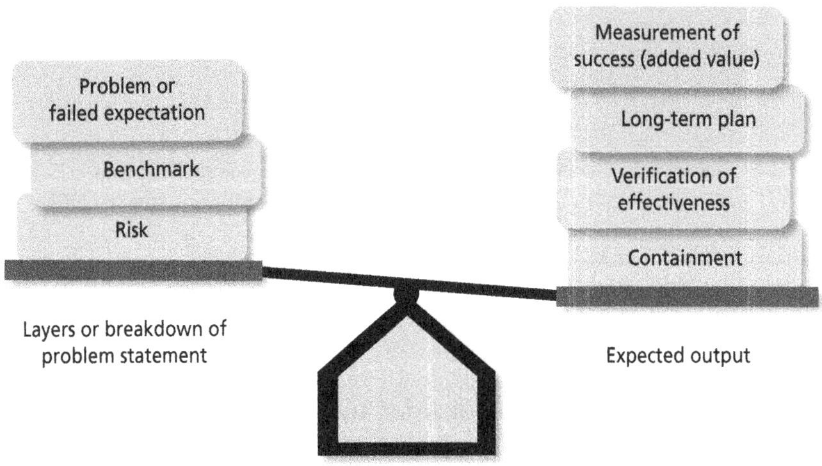

Figure 11.3 Breakdown of the problem statement and expected output.

Example 11.1 Identify the true problem.

Due to repetitive process delays, an independent audit was done to observe the process. It was noted that some operators were taking extended breaks. These breaks were not captured on time cards; therefore, records gave the impression that the lost time was part of the available man hours. The operator delay, in most cases, was about five minutes needed to return to the assembly line to start the process. The five-minute delay may seem insignificant, but if there are, for example, five operators doing this practice twice a day for the three shifts throughout the year, the impact on process cycle time and productivity could be enormous. To add a twist to this example, the operators were taking longer breaks because of the waiting time to use the microwave in the break room. Most of the operators preferred a warmed meal for lunch, especially during the cold seasons, therefore the need for the microwave. So, with this information, what really caused the delay in the process?

Lesson Learned:

If you cannot change the metric, do not measure it! It is a waste of time; measure something else. It is not uncommon to find that the process owners gathering the metrics are unaware of the strategy in place as shown in this example. One way to prevent this waste is to increase visibility of metrics to appropriate teams (e.g., displayed on bulletin boards or announced weekly via email). If metrics are not shared for review, then it is an expensive way of utilizing record keepers.

This simple scenario is an example of a problem that may have hidden causes that can only be uncovered through a structured and in-depth root cause analysis. Understanding the true problem or root cause will help implement the right corrective action.

Solution:

After installing more microwaves and staggering the lunch hours, delays caused by the microwave line were alleviated.

Breaking down the layers of the problem statement provides a better chance with designing the matching expected output. The other benefit of this strategy is the facilitation of benchmarking, the measurement of current status versus the desired success level. It is, therefore, crucial to clearly define the measurable benchmark deliverables during the development of the problem statement so as to provide an accurate measurement of success for the desired output. The selection of the key process indicator (KPI) is dependent on the accuracy of the problem statement. It will be a disaster if data collection and data mining are geared towards the wrong indicators. Variables will be unique for every situation, thus it is also important to recognize basic problem identification tools to start this process.

12

Other Triggers of Root Cause Analysis

MORE THAN NON-CONFORMANCES

Root cause analysis is often missed as an opportunity to improve performance as well as generate savings. This is due to the limited application of this powerful tool on error containment or analysis of customer complaints. Optimization of this tool is overlooked and root cause analysis stays hidden and only brought to the limelight during process disturbance, such as process failure. This reactive approach has overshadowed the other bright side of root cause analysis, which in many cases is an easy strategy to accomplish and generate improvement and savings. Root cause analysis has triggers other than non-conformances, and realization of this notion is the key to the full utilization of this tool to its maximum potential. Examples of these root cause analysis triggers are:

- External forces (e.g., competition affecting market share)
- Internal processes (e.g., compliant processes but no longer competitive)
- Non-conformance or variance

ROOT CAUSE ANALYSIS TRIGGER: EXTERNAL FORCES

Generation of savings using root cause analysis is not a new principle, as it has been implemented in many aspects of the industries for generations. Whenever the food industries perform taste tests for a new or modified product, root cause analysis is at work; testing certain flavors at certain time of the year using a population segment uncovers the root cause that will make the product gain market acceptance or rejection under certain preference indicators. When a medical device manufacturing company validates the efficacy of its products, root cause analysis is a critical tool for a successful approval of its product. Root cause analysis provides data to identify success factors for the key variables that will impact the life cycle of the project.

ROOT CAUSE ANALYSIS TRIGGER: INTERNAL PROCESSES

Root cause analysis can also be triggered by internal processes, in a smaller scale compared to the external triggers discussed above. This type of trigger is probably easier to control and to correct in comparison with external forces. Before a trigger can be addressed, a detection mechanism is first needed to automatically 'flash a sign' announcing the presence of a potential risk or failure. This mechanism is like a train light signal; the railroad sensor detects the on-coming train and the flashing lights are turned on as visible warning signs to prevent an accident. Root cause analysis can work in the same principle by providing alert systems so appropriate action plans can be devised to divert a possible failure path into an improvement opportunity.

The 'warning light' (which is the performance metric) is not limited to high risk failure modes, but also for early detection of the slow process deterioration that has 'outgrown' its original intent and can no longer be competitive. A process with this performance level may be tolerated as long as it is providing minimum revenue until a phase out is finalized. On the other hand, the deteriorating process may have been salvaged and transformed into a growing initiative or phased out sooner for cost effectiveness if there had been an early warning sign to alert the root cause analysis system.

The deployment of root cause analysis as an immediate response to the performance metric warning signal is not always a top priority. As a matter of fact, in some cases, it is the " least traveled path." Why? Some of the major reasons may be attributed to variables that can be easily corrected, if recognized, such as:

- Lack of visible early detection mechanism (may be due to ineffective or lack of performance metric) to initiate a root cause analysis before a failure occurs. This is an example wherein root cause analysis is associated as a mere tool for error correction, not a proactive preventive tool.
- Lack of "selling" the financial benefit of root cause analysis as tool for savings and improvement generation to strengthen management support of the program.
- Lack of workforce understanding and embrace of the culture promoting root cause analysis as an improvement tool rather than a 'finger-pointing' blame weapon.

The good news is that variables listed can easily be 'reversed' to reap the full benefits of a successful root cause analysis in the company's continuous improvement and growth. With this strategy, the root cause analysis program has the opportunity to transform its image from a plain investigation tool into an improvement catalyst and savings generator. The next big challenge is the creation of a strategy and effective deployment program that will self-sustain and withstand the day-to-day processes, customer changes, and stakeholder expectations under a quick-change-over time table. How can this shifting of priorities be achieved and still keep the process performance at the highest level? *Roots* and *wings* are the answers to this challenge. Roots from management support to strengthen the program to withstand constant changes and operational demands; and wings to sustain itself through the grassroots level embrace of the culture. It sounds simple because it is simple. This publication will provide models to understand, create, implement, and verify the effectiveness of root cause analysis for savings generation. Root cause analysis per se is static and does not have the robustness to propel itself in a dynamic mode needed to keep the program energized and maintain self-sustainability. Basic lean tools will be incorporated with the root cause analysis models depicted in this publication to invigorate this system and maximize its power. The lean tools applied in this publication are simple and easy to use with no requirement to have a Black Belt certification. It is no more complicated than the root cause analysis process, with the integration of simple tools to help quantify the current state and the expectations; thus, decisions may be based on measured risks.

ROOT CAUSE ANALYSIS TRIGGER: NONCONFORMANCE OR VARIANCE *(FRIEND OR FOE?)*

Variance detected within the internal operational scope typically requires less expensive containment. All employees should be empowered to identify any potential operational variance based on known standards or guiding principles as they are the subject experts within their areas of responsibility. Being at the grassroots level, the process owners have the visibility and opportunity to prevent these variances from reaching the customers.

Variances discovered outside the operational scope (such as customer complaint or regulatory finding) may be perceived at a higher severity as these variances escaping internal controls pose an unknown risk to the customer. With this unknown risk, it is possible that mitigation cost may rise exponentially (such as expediting a replacement for a returned product at premium cost) to pacify an irate customer and maintain a good customer perception.

Variances appear in many forms. Recognition of symptoms should trigger a root cause analysis to address the variances. Most of the symptoms of variance are typically known to the process owners as they have day-to-day encounters with the operational variables such as material, equipment, policies, and recurring roadblocks. The benefits of internal discovery and immediate reporting of variances are obvious, but what could be the reason for the system's failure to optimize this opportunity? Table 12.1 lists some reasons.

Figure 12.1 shows a comparison between a traditional method of variance or non-conformance evaluation and a lean-based method. The significant difference is the lean-based method of focusing on verification beyond compliance. Compliance is mandatory; without it, there is no benchmark to measure progress. Verification beyond compliance seeks for areas of improvement beyond compliance as these initiatives will ultimately enhance compliance.

Table 12.1 Examples of symptoms of variances.

Symptoms of variances	Possible root cause
Workforce achievements do not meet management expectations	Vision may not be fully understood, therefore not relayed properly to the workforce.
Metrics do not give measurements of the elements *'that matter to customers and stakeholders'*	Process metrics may not be aligned with the company's strategies and objectives.
Waste and performance deterioration are gradually overcoming the system	Process metrics do not reveal the hidden factories.
Recurring errors	Errors undetected by internal controls. Inappropriate metrics. Errors may have been *quick-fixed* but true root cause not identified, therefore error re-occurs.
Demand exceeds capability, hidden by rework, overtime, etc.	Poor planning and ineffective management of leaders.
High resource turnover causing delays and error due to unstable learning curve	Job function not clearly defined leading to constant failure and ultimately to employee turnover. Lack of leadership to motivate employees.
High rate of new account fall out	Contract review process is ineffective in identifying customer expectations. Poor assessment of capability and capacity to support demand; poor planning.

Variance from standard process is almost always accompanied by waste. One simple lean-based tool depicted in Figure 12.2 is the Wheel of Wastes. It is used for the identification of associated wastes which, if minimized, will contribute not only to the reduction of variance but also to savings and the streamlining of the process. Therefore, discovery of a variance is not always a negative event, as it may trigger positive results with the right tools and right attitude. This is a savings opportunity!

As one TV comedian said, *"If life gives you lemons, make lemonade!"* This holds true with variance detection.

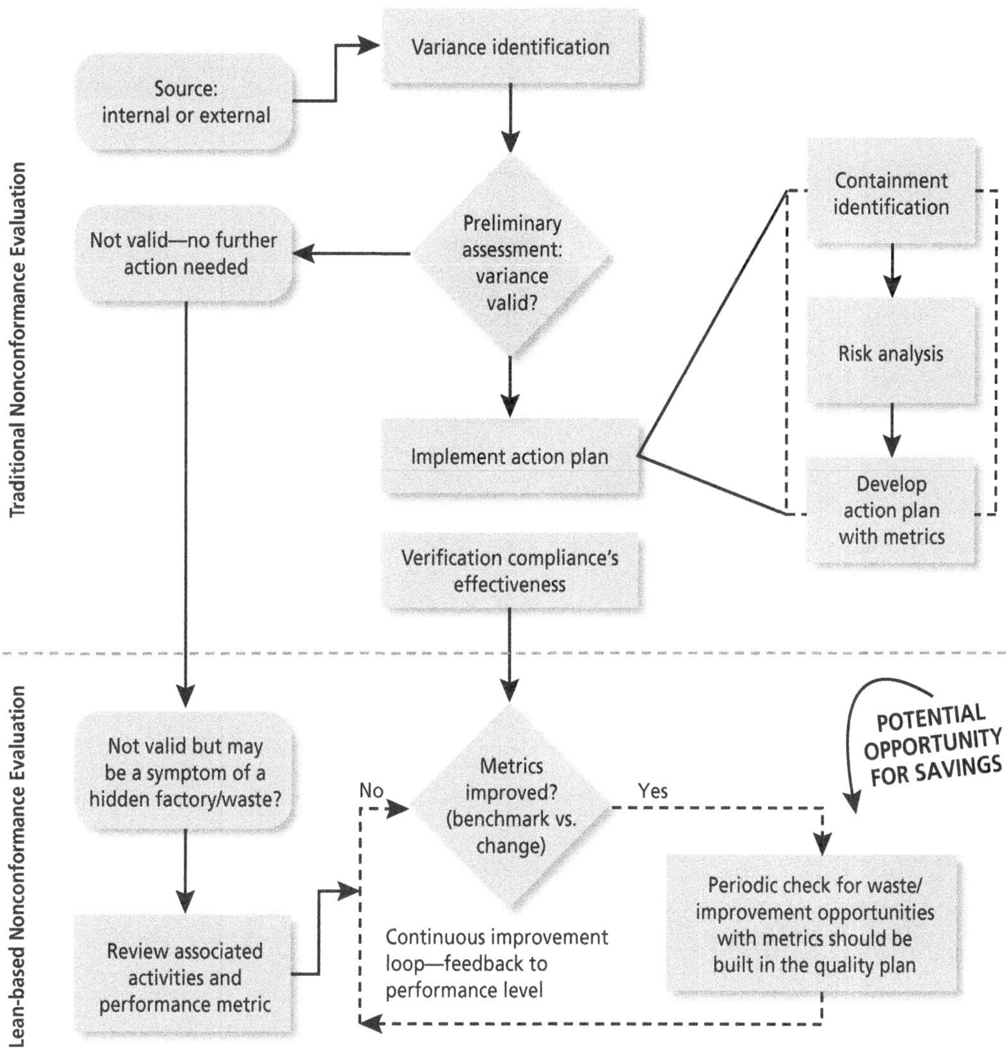

Figure 12.1 Detection of variance as indicator of performance level.

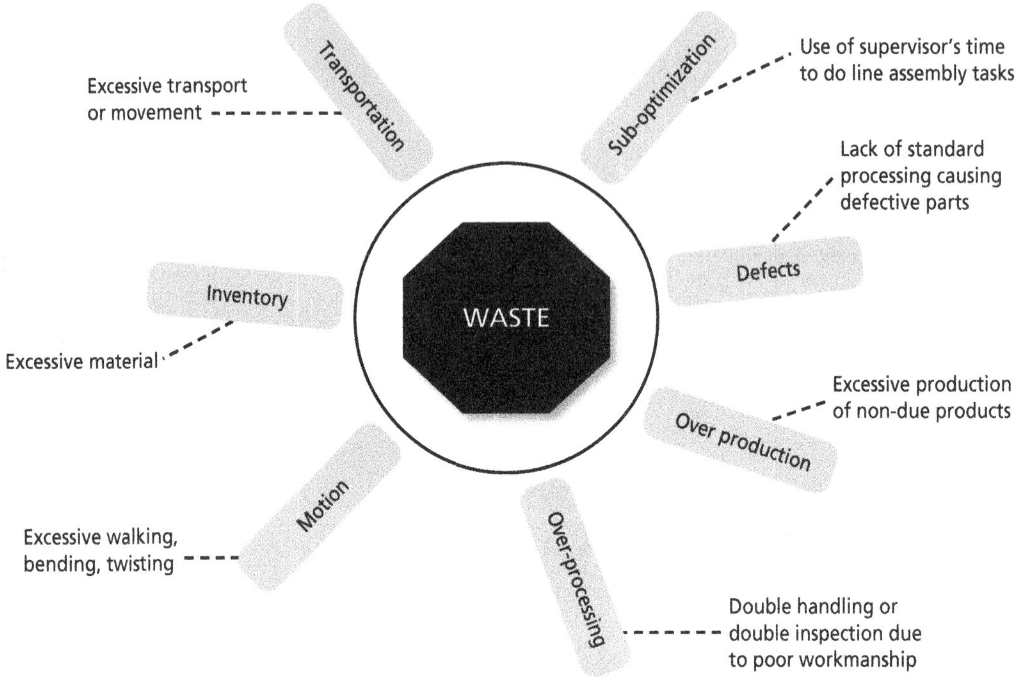

Figure 12.2 Wheel of waste and examples.

13
Root Causes and Process Metrics

WHICH CAME FIRST?

Effective root cause analysis should equate, at minimum, to customer satisfaction and added value if there are improvement and savings as by-products. This is one of the challenges faced by the improvement teams as some root cause analysis results are sometimes vague and not measurable for effectiveness. This static mode is also one of the many reasons why root cause analysis fails as a source of savings. A dynamic root cause analysis, on the other hand, normally triggers a measurable deliverable. The measurement of success will be dependent on the situation, therefore no single template can be used as a default measurement for a problem type; however, the measurement of success should have a correlation with the problem statement and the action plans designed to contain or resolve the issue.

Some of the main guidelines in choosing the right measurements of success are:

- Problem statement should identify the current situation *(where you are)* and the expected future state *(where you want to be)*.
- Root cause should identify cause of the gap between current and desired state that caused the problem.
- Measure of success should be using the metrics to close the gap discovered during the analysis and sustain progress.

This module aims to heighten the awareness on the recognition of the differences between a stagnant and a dynamic measurable root cause analysis as shown in Table 13.1 through Table 13.10, through the analysis of sample problem statements.

The strategy of conveying information through concrete examples is sometimes more effective than theoretical explanation of concepts. The focus is to show examples of possible metrics of success, but not limited to the listing, which are often missed during the analysis process. The input elements and expected results will dictate the metrics.

Table 13.1 Root cause and process metrics example: late delivery.

Problem Reported: Late delivery.	
Method 1: Dynamic, with Measure of Success	**Method 2: Stagnant, without Metrics**
Root Cause: Delivery delayed by traffic accident.	**Root Cause:** Delivery delayed by traffic accident.
Action: Review of performance data for last 6 months showed on target, 99% on-time delivery, supporting conclusion that this is isolated.	**Action:** Freight expedited to address customer dissatisfaction.
Measure of Action's Success: Recommended performance metric • Expedite cost due to late delivery *(this is an indicator of exception frequency; upward trend should prompt an investigation as the exceptions, such as traffic issues, should not become part of the norm).*	**Measure of Action's Success:** This is considered an uncontrollable and isolated incident; no further action.

Table 13.2 Root cause and process metrics example: damaged product.

Problem Reported: Damaged product.	
Method 1: Dynamic, with Measure of Success	**Method 2: Stagnant, without Metrics**
Root Cause: No visible performance measurement as early indicator of training needs/effectiveness.	**Root Cause:** Inappropriate handling by packagers using the new box maker model caused damages on product.
Action: Packagers have been re-trained on the new box maker model and monitoring of training effectiveness has been included in the training program.	**Action:** Packagers have been re-trained on the new equipment model.
Measure of Action's Success: Recommended performance metrics Training the workforce on any skill set does not necessarily mean the knowledge has been absorbed and understood. Training effectiveness should be measured via the following, monitored on a periodic basis: • Error rate *(to verify understanding of process and effectiveness of training).* • Cycle time *(to verify if there is a significant fluctuation between workers as this may be an indication of further training needs).*	**Measure of Action's Success:** Training records verified as completed.

Table 13.3 Root cause and process metrics example: lost shipment.

Problem Reported: Lost shipment.	
Method 1: Dynamic, with Measure of Success	Method 2: Stagnant, without Metrics
Root Cause: Packaging error due to lack of standard back-up process in the event of address scanner failure (i.e., standard manual loading process).	**Root Cause:** Shipment was sent to the wrong customer due to mix-up during packaging (customer address scanner not working and tracking was done manually).
Action: Scanner was fixed, failure mode under evaluation. Back-up manual process has been defined and validated.	**Action:** Scanner was fixed. Shipment has been replaced via claims credit.
Measure of Action's Success: Recommended performance metrics • Downtime frequency of scanner *(to identify severity of scanner issue).* • Claims for lost shipments when manual process is used *(to validate equivalency of the manual and scanning process).* • Error rate resulting from manual process *(to validate accuracy of manual process).*	**Measure of Action's Success:** Scanner upgrade completed; scanning after upgrade was reviewed; no discrepancy noted.

Table 13.4 Root cause and process metrics example: wrong quality declared.

Problem Reported: Wrong quantity declared on shipping manifest.	
Method 1: Dynamic, with Measure of Success	Method 2: Stagnant, without Metrics
Root Cause: Supplier's non-standard packaging practice of taping boxes together resulted in count error during the receiving process.	**Root Cause:** Receiving Operator inadvertently missed one box count because two boxes coming from supplier were taped together, giving the appearance of one box.
Action: Supplier has been notified of the discrepancy to correct future shipments.	**Action:** Receiving Supervisor discussed with Receiving operator the importance of attention to details.
Measure of Action's Success: Recommended performance metric Supplier performance metric to include supplier-controlled variables that can be verified by Receiving—examples: integrity of packaging, quality level, quantity, on-time delivery, etc. *(this is to verify consistency of supplier's performance; start of a declining trend needs to evaluated to ensure metric of acceptance remains positive).*	**Measure of Action's Success:** Training records and documentation of discussion with operator verified and completed.

Table 13.5 Root cause and process metrics example: exceeded overtime budget.

<table>
<tr><th colspan="2">Problem Reported: Shipping Department exceeded the approved customer overtime budget over a period of one month due to unexpected volume increase.</th></tr>
<tr><th>Method 1: Dynamic, with Measure of Success</th><th>Method 2: Stagnant, without Metrics</th></tr>
<tr><td>Root Cause: Change management has no advance process indicator to alert the system on major changes (e.g., volume increase) so containment and proactive resolution can be developed.</td><td>Root Cause: Additional manpower (overtime) was needed to complete the unexpected volume increase.</td></tr>
<tr><td>Action: Review of change management will be evaluated to include key process indicators as proactive measures.</td><td>Action: Additional manpower will be hired to eliminate overtime to address volume increase.</td></tr>
<tr><td>Measure of Action's Success: Recommended metrics
• Capability versus demand (capability available needs to be visible to ensure compatibility with demand volume and time frame).
• Overtime (this is a possible indication of a variation in demand, capability, etc.—start of a trend needs to be investigated).
• Cycle time (baseline should be defined so this metric can be used as indicator of a variation occurrence; results beyond the process tolerance should be investigated).</td><td>Measure of Action's Success: Hiring completion verified. Overtime showed lower hours during the follow-up audit.</td></tr>
</table>

Table 13.6 Root cause and process metrics example: international freight delays.

Problem Reported: International freight arrived on time at US port but was left on US port causing delay of delivery to customer.	
Method 1: Dynamic, with Measure of Success	**Method 2: Stagnant, without Metrics**
Root Cause: Hand-off flow from international-to-domestic delivery needs clarification to enhance effectiveness and additional error-proofing.	**Root Cause:** Operators at the US port inadvertently left the freight at the dock due to mix-up.
Action: Hand-off process was audited to verify roadblocks and improvement opportunities.	**Action:** Supervisor responsible for US port discussed the importance of timely sorting and delivery.
Measure of Action's Success: Recommended performance metrics • Cycle time *(to identify if certain accounts are more complex than others so proper resource/window time can be allocated; shorter window time may have caused 'rushing' of completing tasks and may potentially cause errors and mix-up).* • Error rate *(to verify consistency of quality performance; start of a trend should be evaluated).*	**Measure of Action's Success:** Evidence of supervisor's meeting with operators regarding reiteration of procedure compliance verified and completed.

Table 13.7 Root cause and process metrics example: delivery damaged.

Problem Reported: Rolls of upholstery material always delivered damaged.	
Method 1: Dynamic, with Measure of Success	**Method 2: Stagnant, without Metrics**
Root Cause: Best practice for loading of rolls was not validated for effectiveness prior to account's release to operations.	**Root Cause:** Loading operators drag the rolls with the tip of the forklift during loading as there is no equipment suitable to carry the long heavy rolls. This technique damages the rolls.
Action: • Best practice technique will be evaluated. • Issue discussed with supplier to evaluate cost effectiveness of better packaging to protect product and facilitate ease of transport.	**Action:** Operators were instructed to put rolls on pallets to prevent damage occurrence.
Measure of Action's Success: Recommended performance metrics • Perform risk analysis *(revenue generation from this account versus damage cost versus purchase of correct loading equipment)* • Damage occurrence before and after implementation of best practice and supplier packaging modification *(to monitor if actions are effective).*	**Measure of Action's Success:** The next shipment was successfully delivered and accepted by the customer.

Table 13.8 Root cause and process metrics example: shift productivity differential.

Problem Reported: The second-shift operators seem more productive than the first-shift operators.	
Method 1: Dynamic, with Measure of Success	**Method 2: Stagnant, without Metrics**
Root Cause: Volume workload and manpower allocation are the same for both first and second shift; therefore, handling units processed are the same for both shifts. However, the first-shift operators have devised a faster methodology to shorten the cycle time and still maintain the required quality level, leaving ample time for break.	**Root Cause:** First-shift operators take longer breaks than the second-shift operators.
Action: First-shift operators were acknowledged as innovators and were given the privilege to share lesson learned with second shift to streamline their process. Workload/resource allocation adjusted to optimize resources.	**Action:** First-shift operators were reprimanded for taking long breaks and were given performance warning.
Measure of Action's Success: Recommended performance metrics • Cycle time *(benchmark should be established; significant variation should be evaluated).* • Productivity measure *(to measure output versus expectations; extreme fluctuations should be investigated).* • Capability/Capacity measures *(to verify resource allocation and use)*	**Measure of Action's Success:** Clock in/out to monitor operator time and breaks. (This is policing work and does not add value).

Table 13.9 Root cause and process metrics example: paperwork errors.

Problem Reported: Material release paperwork error consistently occurs during weekend shift.	
Method 1: Dynamic, with Measure of Success	Method 2: Stagnant, without Metrics
Root Cause: Tools to aid the non-regular weekend operators need clarification to better guide operators on rotation during weekends.	**Root Cause:** Operators not normally assigned in the process are rotated to perform weekend shifts.
Action: Tools to guide weekend operators have been developed: • Work instructions for material release • Identification of training needs and verification of effectiveness	**Action:** Appropriate training for the rotation team has been completed.
Measure of Action's Success: Recommended performance metrics Internal monitoring of weekend work for a duration at the discretion of the Supervisor to validate the process: • Cycle time of weekend work versus regular day work *(to assess proper resource allocation)* • Internal error rate via internal sampling until confidence level is satisfied	**Measure of Action's Success:** Customer feedback *(this is a reactive action and not preventive).*

Table 13.10 Root cause and process metrics example: wait time and production delay.

Problem Reported: Long waiting time for incoming truck drivers to unload freight at dock causing production delay.	
Method 1: Dynamic, with Measure of Success	**Method 2: Stagnant, without Metrics**
Root Cause: Two primary causes: • Delivery window times from suppliers are not scheduled, causing long queue and delay at receiving dock. • No cycle time measurement for unloading each trailer to determine proper resource allocation.	**Root Cause:** Not enough operators to unload the incoming freight to expedite the process.
Action: Schedule delivery times for major suppliers and start cycle time study to assess resource allocation.	**Action:** Additional operators have been hired to expedite unloading of incoming freight.
Measure of Action's Success: Recommended performance metrics • Trailer queue time from point of arrival to time of unloading *(to verify waiting time, causing delay).* • Trailer unloading cycle time *(to verify efficiency of internal process; inefficiency will possibly contribute to delay).*	**Measure of Action's Success:** Internal customer feedback *(this is reactive and may be biased opinion).*

LESSONS LEARNED (A LASTING IMPRESSION)

The following examples are fictitious events. Sometimes, peculiar examples such as these leave a lasting impression to emphasize lessons learned. This style may also be used as a communication tool in relaying critical messages to the grassroots workers.

Example 13.1 Backhoe wheelie.

Problem Reported:

Preventive maintenance records of a very stable backhoe showed excessive repairs during summer months for the last three years. Repair records were traced to one particular piece of equipment and one specific summer temporary worker. Observation of job performance did not show any anomaly.

Investigation results:

During one on-site observation after the job completion, it was noted that the summer temporary worker invited friends to watch him do a "backhoe wheelie" (raising one or both front tires while the backhoe was running, simulating a motorcycle creative riding, shown in Figure 13.1). This creates excessive strain on the backhoe, as it is not meant for this purpose. This anomaly was hard to detect as it was being done right after job completion, lasting for only a few minutes. However, this repeated abuse of the equipment during the summer months led to the deterioration of the equipment.

Figure 13.1 Backhoe wheelie caught on camera.

Root cause:

- There was no sufficient process control to prevent abuse or improper use of the equipment.

Action plan should be focused on the root cause, examples:

- Policies regarding proper use of the material should be part of the labor contract.
- On-site supervision needs to be reviewed to address equipment put-away policy.

Example 13.2 Sleeping on the job.

Problem Reported:

An innovative business called *Dogs Rule* provides highly trained watchdogs to patrol high-security buildings. During the first months of operation, the company's service performance seemed effective. Lately, there have been complaints on the security failure in preventing trespassers from loitering in the property.

Investigation results:

Dogs Rule company sent an auditor to visit one of the patrolled sites to find the root cause of the service failure. The auditor took this picture, which explained the security failure.

Photographer: Janet Bautista Smith, Downtown, San Luis Potosi, Mexico

Figure 13.2 Watchdog caught on camera, sleeping on the job.

Root causes:

- Failure of the company to listen to the VOC (voice of the customer), including non-verbal expectations (i.e., watch dog needs to be fully alert during shift).
- Lack of cross check to ensure fully rested dogs are sent on rotation.

Action plan should be focused on the root cause, examples:

- Watch dogs rotation log was put in place to monitor shift watch hours to ensure fully rested dogs are put in assignment.
- Spot checking of the watch dog's performance was also implemented to traffic flow in the area, to further align the watch dog's patrol schedule.

PART IV
Auditing

14
Auditing

VERIFYING COMPLIANCE, PERFORMANCE, AND CONTINUOUS IMPROVEMENT OPPORTUNITY

Auditing is one of the critical tools essential for the heartbeat of the business but often hidden behind the scenes and not given the deserved acknowledgement. It is like an unpolished gem waiting to be discovered so it can display its glimmer. In most cases, it is stashed away somewhere as if it is an heirloom that is kept away from the public view. Why is it this way?

Some professionals in this function do not always know how to "polish" this gem to make it shine like a precious jewel; they may be very focused on getting the job done and not worried about accolade. This is a benevolent approach; however, the leverage of highlighting the audit program to 'sell' the concept of using the audit program as an improvement and savings generator is not optimized. The traditional outlook of the audit function by some segments of the industry is that of a necessity, like a medication taken to sustain the health of the system. This perception was probably part of an older style of passive audit program. This style has no energetic waves emanating from the audit results to stir the stillness of *'status quo'* into a vibrant transformation called improvement changes. This phase is challenging to achieve and, in some cases, very difficult to succeed as there are many operational roadblocks and silos along the way preventing the smooth flow. This difficulty may be compounded by other variables that lie within the center of the quality audit management. Lack of exposure to other tools may hinder the audit role's visibility as a catalyst for improvement. Under this situation, oftentimes audit results are addressed by merely correcting the non-conformances identified without further initiatives on the improvement aspect of the system. The stakeholders' business interest is not just the achievement of compliance, but also profit improvement and growth to sustain the continuing demand for customer satisfaction. With this said, the quality focus should not be limited to compliance, but should be extended to the continuing improvement and sustainability of the system.

This publication will demonstrate strategies in achieving these goals through the integration of basic quality tools, specifically Lean Six Sigma (LSS), to align the audit program with the company's vision and strategic planning. With this roadmap, the internal audit program will become intertwined with the main flow of the business rather than an isolated element disconnected from the system. It is important that the internal audit program is in parallel with the company's priorities and direction to maximize the full potential of the auditing role in verifying not just the compliance aspect but the initiatives' effectiveness. If not aligned with the business direction, the audit program may be exerting efforts and resources on priorities different from management's expectations. Thus, it is crucial that this alignment exists to continually support the output desired by the stakeholders.

LEAN SIX SIGMA

Does one need to be a Six Sigma Black Belt to implement these tools? And why choose Lean Six Sigma as the implementation engine?

One does not have to be a Lean expert to execute the tools demonstrated in this module. As with any other tool set, the simplicity or complexity of the tool selection is dependent on the needs. This module presents basic principles and easy-to-apply methodologies to demonstrate that the application of these tools will aid in the promotion of the audit results as catalyst for improvement. This initiative will further highlight the audit function's added value and recognition as a critical tool for improvement. What is the best route for this initiative?

As with any operational program, there are many ways to help transform the audit function into a dynamic partner to achieve operational goals. One is the DMAIC path explained in Figure 14.1. This concept is one of the many models helpful in the transformation of a compliance audit to a measurable improvement initiative.

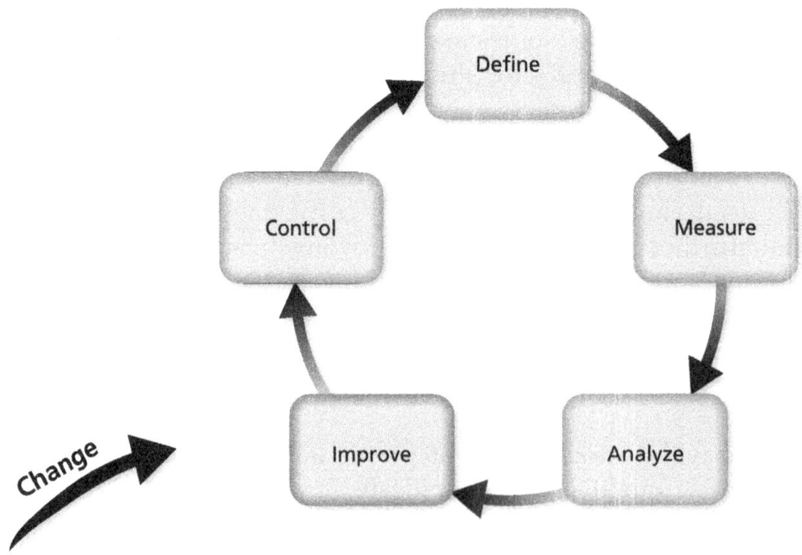

Figure 14.1 Dynamic quality audit model: measurable results to trigger movement.

CREATION OF A DYNAMIC AUDIT ROADMAP

This lean-based audit model facilitates the optimization of the audit elements in generating improvement and saving.

Scope of the Audit

Implementation of the lean-focused internal audit may be challenging to the 'one-track' mentality of focusing only on compliance and inadvertently ignoring the potential improvement opportunities. It is common to hear these statements: *"We have so many complaints for this process; let us audit and ensure all workers are following the procedures"* or *"There so many errors; the workers are not following procedures."*

Following all the written procedures 100% may sound good, but this may not be enough to error-proof the process. Maybe the process has evolved and is no longer compatible with its environment and the other variables associated with the process. If this is the case, 100% compliance with the written procedures will be futile since the procedures are no longer effective. Sometimes, this 'evolution' is caused by small incremental changes that are not noticeable as the impact is so small, but cumulatively these changes have a significant impact on the process. One example is the wide tolerance setting and low preventive maintenance for a non-critical stable process. Then one day, the customer changes the product specification to a tighter tolerance due to market demand. In this example, the workers may be following the procedures 100% but the process capability and customer requirements are no longer compatible—possibly resulting in instability and random errors. Auditing the process focusing only on compliance may not catch this improvement opportunity.

This is the beauty of the lean-focused audit—it does not depend solely on procedural compliance. Other variables that impact the input and output of the process are taken into consideration, increasing the chances of identifying the true condition of the process.

The lean-focused audit foundation includes:

- Added value to all involved stakeholders (i.e., customer satisfaction, company financial strength, workforce development, and process improvement)
- Conversion of root cause analysis into corrective actions and measurable initiatives as feedback to the system
- Provision of basic tools in sustaining the process beyond compliance and continuous improvement

There needs to be a balance between compliance and 'thinking-out-of the box' to identify improvement opportunities. Focusing only on compliance will curb the system's ability to see the other side of non-compliance, which is the opportunity for improvement. Once the audit program defines the problem or gap, the next big step is the root cause analysis. This method requires a creative mind and understanding of the system to fully analyze the different variables, sometimes hidden from view, that are causing the problem.

Pinpointing the root cause of a nonconformance possibly caused by a non-distinct element such as an error triggered by human intervention is a challenging task. It is sometimes easy to just say, *"It was due to human error; humans are not perfect, and we are allowed to make mistakes."* Is "human error" an acceptable justification for a discrepancy? In general, the answer is *no.*

Human error, in most cases, has a reason other than human intervention. In any process, it's possible to dissect the elements associated with human intervention by analyzing the root causes of the variables affecting the *"human intervention."* Here are some examples based on the 6Ms lean concept:

Process capability

- Is the process too complex, with unclear direction, and therefore prone to error?
- Has the process reached its maximum capability and technology limit, therefore variation beyond control is likely to occur?
- Has there been any major change to impact fit, form, and function?

System

- Is the system fully optimized in providing support to the human activities such as sufficient training and verification of training effectiveness?
- Are there clear procedures or visual standards to help prevent errors?

Manpower planning

- Is there proper resource allocation to ensure peak volume is fully supported?
- Is there proper training provided by the system?

Machine maintenance

- Is the equipment capable to meet the requirements?
- Is there an acceptable equipment preventive maintenance program to eliminate sub-standard equipment processing of products, ultimately impacting error rate?

Method

- Is the process or method repeatable (proven by validation)? If this is an unstable process, failure is likely to occur, not necessarily due to human intervention.
- Is there measurement or indicator to detect potential failure? If so, is there a containment or escalation method?

Material

- Is the material stable, properly released for production use?
- Has there been any change that may cause impact on the process?

Other business partner processes

- Has there been any change with supplier processes?

These are just a few of the operational elements that may be the true root causes of 'human error.' These elements may remain covered in the hidden factories if the root cause analysis methodology does not dig deep enough to expose these issues. In some cases, these issues are missed due to the narrow-mindedness of the system in focusing mainly on compliance. This situation can be corrected through the introduction of various tools in root cause analysis (such as 5-whys, 8-Ds, fishbone, and others). With management support and proper workforce training, this cultural change can be easily achieved. However, the other reason for missing these hidden factories is the most difficult one to reverse: that is the intentional creation of internal silos to perpetuate the existence of hidden factories for personal gain. Hopefully, this type of mind-set is rare. It may be uncommon, but this type of unit does exist in the business world. Fear not as there are countermeasures to prevent, detect, and correct this circle. One solution is the creation of a dynamic audit model that will give the system the ability to drill down and see through the different layers of the system.

To fully explain the application of this lean-based audit model, see Figure 14.2.

Note: The sample findings in the following examples are not inclusive for the standard used as audit requirement. The sample findings are audit fragments to show the conversion of sample compliance audit findings into measurable process improvement and possible savings, as well as a dynamic feedback mechanism to the process.

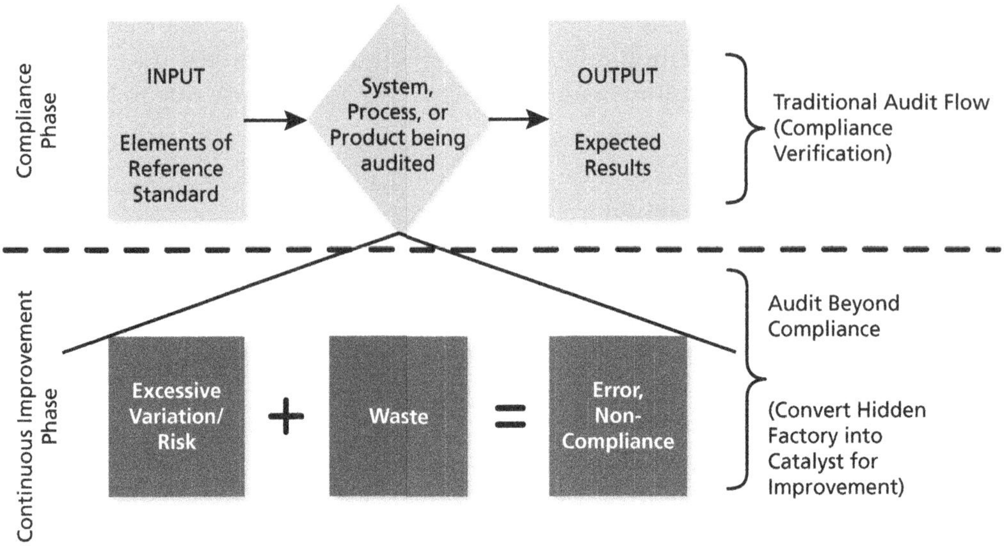

Figure 14.2 Auditing beyond compliance model.

Reference: Presentation by Janet Bautista-Smith, *Strategic Planning and Systems Thinking: Roadmap to Sustainable Quality Beyond Compliance,* ASQ 2012 National Quality Education Conference, KY.

AUDITING BEYOND COMPLIANCE MODEL

The following audit examples are not meant to be conclusive for the elements used in the examples below. The purpose of the examples is to show the differences between the typical compliance audit versus lean-based audit observed by the author in her more than 25 years of experience auditing for manufacturing industries under the governance of the FDA, military, aerospace, automotive, telecommunications, and general commercial businesses. The examples show how auditing beyond compliance can help convert action plans into long-term improvement and savings.

The observations noted under each example may be a fraction of the overall observations applicable for the elements used as examples. The example findings are condensed in nature and cited to show conversion of a possibly stagnant plan into dynamic measurable initiatives. One may ask, in some cases, whether the auditor has limited information about the different metrics that may have significant impact on savings, and therefore may not necessarily be uncovered during audit. Because auditors are not supposed to be 'consultants,' another question may be asked: How can the auditors identify these measurable savings by generating metrics?

The answer is simple. Ask the process owners these key performance metrics trigger questions:

- Are there controls or procedures in place so they know they are giving expected output?

- How is the process owner alerted by the system for an early detection of a possible non-conformance or failure?
- How does the process owner know that the action is effective?

There are many versions of answers to these simple questions and it is important that the auditor does not get lost in the myriad of information that the process owner may provide during the audit.

A simple performance metric for each of the critical or core processes will answer these questions. The process owners need to define these metrics as they are the subject experts of their field and have vast knowledge of the related processes associated with their tasks. The audit function is the trigger to evaluate compliance and effectiveness of these metrics. By asking the above questions, the audit function is not just performing compliance verification, but also providing an added value in helping the process owners analyze their system and provide the needed information to help define or adjust the metrics for their system.

Example 14.1 Process to be audited: quote flow (see Figure 14.3).

Ref: ISO 9001:2015 Element 4.4.1 Quality Management System

"c. Determine criteria and methods needed to ensure the effective operation and control of these processes."

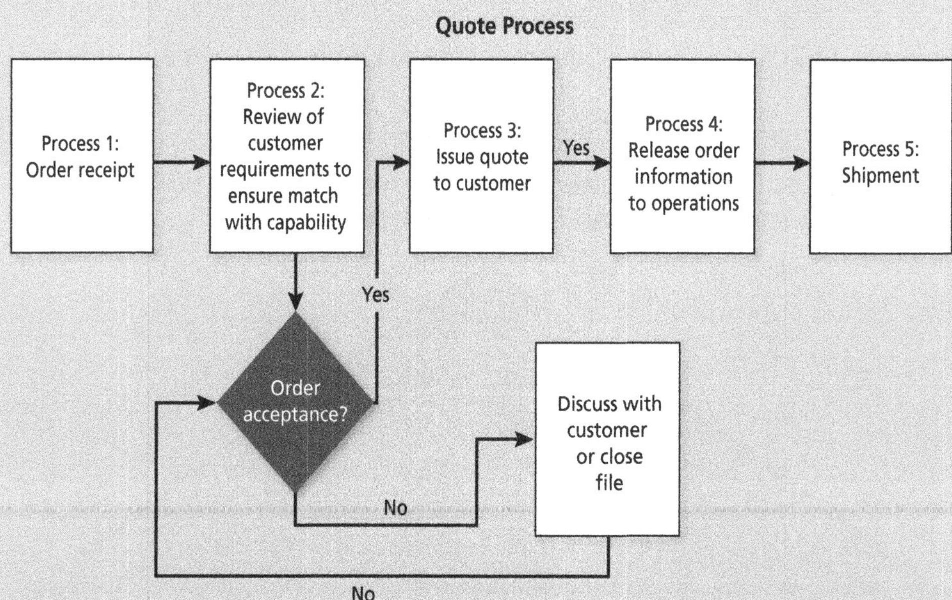

Figure 14.3 Audit process example: quote flow.

Example of Compliance Audit Report:

Chart indicates process flow, review of customer requirements versus capability match, and clear-cut decision points. No discrepancy noted.

Lean-based additional comment to the compliance audit above:

Chart shows process flow reviewed showed no discrepancy; however, there is no program to show effectiveness of quote process. There are many ways to measure effectiveness of the program. Some sample metrics are:

a. Cycle time of quote receipt-to-release
b. Operations start-up timeline versus customer requirement (any delay due to incomplete information during quote?)

Conversion of action initiatives into process metrics and measurable savings:

Savings opportunities—

The two metrics (cycle time and operations start up) may possibly help properly allocate resources (prevention of overtime):

a. Cycle time of quote process versus available manpower
b. Trend of late shipments due to delays that could have been addressed during quoting

Example 14.2 Process to be audited: document control hierarchy and sample records of resource allocation planning (see Figure 14.4).

Ref: ISO 9001:2015 Element 7.5.1 Documented information

"b. documented information determined by the organization as being necessary for the effectiveness of the quality management system."

Figure 14.4 Audit process example: document control hierarchy.

Example of Compliance Audit Report:

There is evidence that the Company Mission and quality policy/objectives are documented and communicated. No discrepancy noted.

Lean-based additional comment to the compliance audit above:

There are no documented method or objective evidence to assess or measure effectiveness of the quality management system.

Conversion of action initiatives into process metrics and measurable savings:

Savings opportunities—

- Measure of effectiveness for the core elements of the quality management system should be clearly defined.
- Identify/minimize associated waste and evaluate progress via the established method of measurement..

Example 14.3 Process sampled during the audit: process performance chart of process X (see Figure 14.5).

Reference: ISO 9001:2015 Element 9.1.3 Analysis and Evaluation

"The organization shall analyze and evaluate appropriate data and information arising from monitoring and measurement. The results of the analysis shall be used to evaluate:

c. the performance and effectiveness of the quality management system."

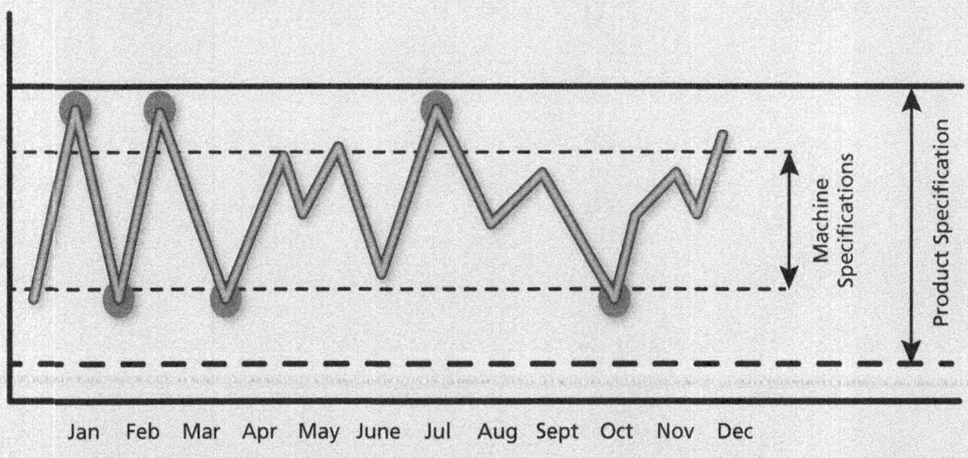

Figure 14.5 Audit process example: performance chart.

Example of Compliance Audit Report:

Process/product performances are monitored, adjustments are documented. Out-of-specification items are segregated for rework per work instructions. No discrepancy noted.

Lean-based additional comment to the compliance audit above:

No formal review of the machine specification versus product specifications.

Products rejected (circled on chart) using machine specifications are within the product specifications. Does the tight machine tolerance need for optimum effectiveness?

Conversion of action initiatives into process metrics and measurable savings:

Savings opportunities—

Figure 14.5 shows opportunity to review and validate the possibility of widening machine tolerance so good products are not rejected.

Costs associated with rejection of good products before and after adjustment of specification (e.g., rework cost, manpower, material, machine availability, etc.).

This cost savings opportunity may not be feasible if the customer requires the tight machine tolerance for reasons such as design sensitivity, high product risk, etc.

Example 14.4 Process to be audited: internal audit program (see Figure 14.6).

Reference: ISO 9001:2015, Element 9.2 – Internal Audit

"The organization shall conduct internal audits at planned intervals to provide information on whether the quality management system:

b. is effectively implemented and maintained."

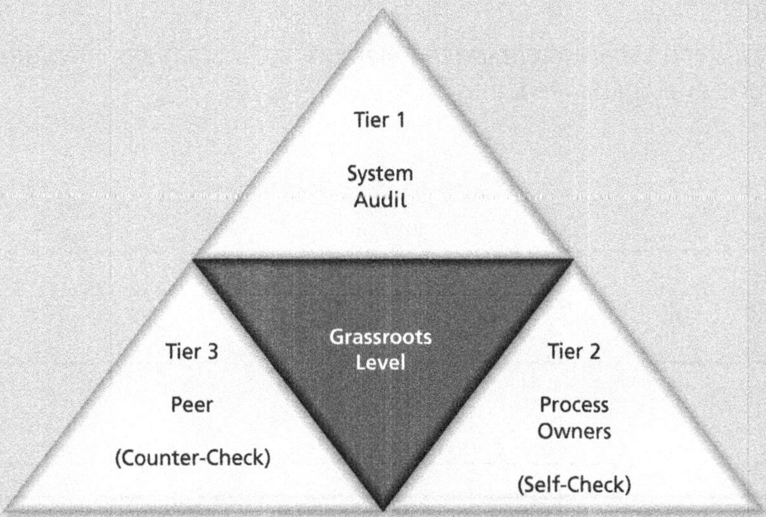

Figure 14.6 Audit process example: internal audit program hierarchy.

Example of Compliance Audit Report:

Audit schedule, audit reports, and follow up are complete within the guidelines of the standard. No discrepancy noted.

Lean-based additional comment to the compliance audit above:

Although the records showed compliance with the requirements of the ISO elements, there is no process indicator to show effectiveness of internal audit in identifying improvement opportunities (not just compliance).

Conversion of action initiatives into process metrics and measurable savings:

Savings opportunities—

Include measurement of improvement savings resulting from internal audit, example: reduced sampling plan for stable suppliers.

Depending on the industry regulation, a company may promote routine grassroots level self-check to increase compliance awareness and the identification of possible compliance issues as an empowerment initiative. This will help increase the surprise findings during audits.

Example 14.5 Process records sampled during audit: machine shutdown and non-conforming product segregation.

Three machine shutdowns occurred due to the three points (circled on chart) out of the specification (see Figure 14.7). These points brought the overall process performance below the acceptable level.

Reference: ISO 9001:2015 Element 9.1 – Monitoring, measurement, analysis and evaluation:

"The organization shall determine the methods for monitoring, measurement, analysis and evaluation needed to ensure valid results."

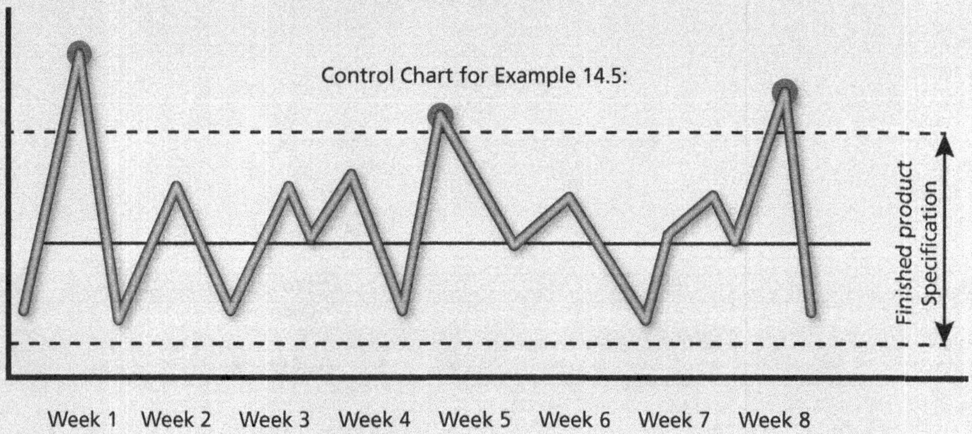

Figure 14.7 Audit process example: control chart.

Example of Compliance Audit Report:

Proper procedure for machine shutdown and non-conforming product segregation were followed during the occurrence of out-of-specification production.

Lean-based additional comment to the compliance audit above:

No program to investigate root causes of special event, to validate start of a trend or a potential outliers or cyclical events (in addition to containment).

Possible outliers or cyclical events may be due to special reasons and not machine related, such as material deviation, operator change, etc.).

Conversion of action initiatives into process metrics and measurable savings:

Savings opportunities—

Identification of outliers or cyclical root causes will prevent or shorten the sometimes costly machine shutdown through the application of the lesson learned prevention plan.

Lesson Learned from this Chapter

A sample checklist for the conversion of audit findings into measurable improvement is illustrated in Table 14.1.

Table 14.1 Audit process checklist.

Improvement Opportunity	Recommended Method of Implementation	Sample Template to Execute the Improvement Initiative
1. Know the company vision and overall strategies	Review of vision interpretation by the workforce during audits	Make vision visible as a living document (display of vision)
2. Identify the major initiatives within each department or process supporting each strategy	Verification of the major initiatives can be made part of the departmental performance metrics.	See Template 14.3 Brainstorming Worksheet for Departmental Performance Metrics
3. Create a dynamic audit roadmap designed to: a. verify compliance with standards governing the company (e.g., ISO) b. verify alignment and performance measurement of initiatives with the business direction (vision and strategies)	The audit roadmap should be incorporated as part of the procedural and quality records system. This will help standardization and visibility of the program.	See Template 14.4 Management Review/ Initiatives – Scorecard of Performance Metrics See Template 14.5 Internal Audit Checklist – Performance Metrics See Templates 14.6 and 14.7 lean tool template (e.g., SIPOC, 5-why) to increase visibility variables impacting process effectiveness (not just compliance).
4. Development of improvement and savings program by converting action plans into measurable results and potential savings using lean tools	Create success factors list for each core process to be verified during audit Waste identification during audits	See Template 14.8 Identification of Roadblocks
5. Sustainability of the improvement plan and continuous growth	The structured continuous improvement program should have a periodic review to ensure continuing alignment and growth. The metrics can be made part of the audit program to provide feedback to the system.	See Template 14.9 Data Collection for Performance Metrics

PART V
Beyond Compliance and Beyond Sustainability

15

Process Metrics: Beyond Compliance, Beyond Sustainability

Before a system can move forward to the next level, compliance must first be achieved as the benchmark. Achievement of compliance does not necessarily mean complete success or achievement of the stakeholder's expectations. The life cycle needs to be sustained to maintain the desired level of operational performance. Then what? Once sustainability checks and balances have been installed and found effective, just like a 'well-oiled machine," then it is time to go to the level beyond performance sustainability. Achievement of this level, in most cases, means opportunity to optimize and deploy resources that would otherwise be exhausted used for 'firefighting' (e.g., rework, sorting, claims due to errors) rather than involvement in added-value programs. Firefighting activities not only deplete the resources but may possibly cause other errors (casualty of the fire) or missed opportunities such as improvement and savings. Consistent maintenance of the desired performance level is an indicator that the metrics were properly designed to provide effective feedback.

Some companies may be perfectly contented with this calm and stable state; however, some companies may optimize this 'peace and quiet' state as a catalyst to go beyond the sustainability level.

Why change the system? *"If it is not broken, why fix it?"* This philosophy means retaining the 'status quo,' which may not work for all cases. Remaining the same, without changes, and producing consistent output may be a goal applicable to some businesses such as a monopoly over certain services or items. As the situation exists, however, a majority of businesses face stiff competition and remaining 'as is' may not be an option. These are some of the many variables in a tight competitive environment that may act as change drivers to the vision:

- Technical innovation
- Expansion through acquisition
- Diversification of service offerings or new product lines
- Outsourcing
- Operational capability / pricing

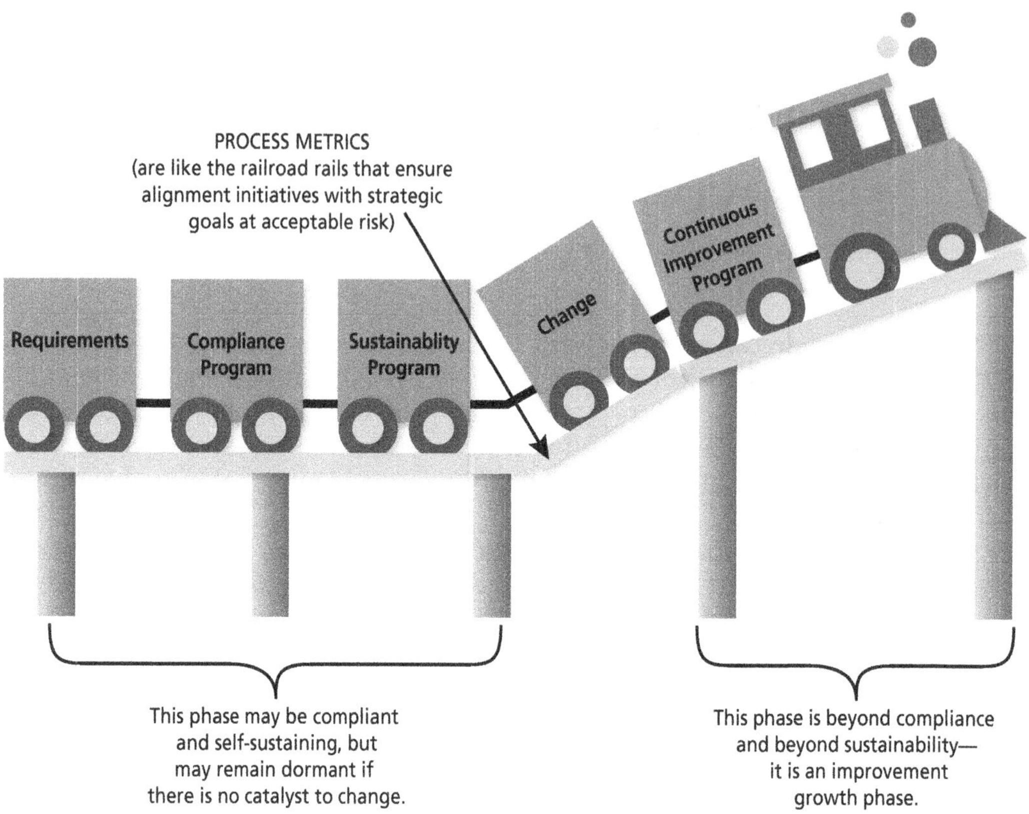

Figure 15.1 Integration of strategic planning, risk, process metrics, and auditing.

Limited funds, resources, and time may be the biggest constraints in the selection of competitive initiatives to remain in the business and achieve profitability. Switching to the latest technology or expanding through acquisition may not be an option that most companies can afford. However, there are less costly ways to compete without sacrificing quality, such as lower pricing or shorter lead. One way is the streamlining of the system/processes for maximum efficiency. One industry accepted methodology is through the implementation of lean-based continuous improvement to generate savings and increase profitability.

A lean-based continuous improvement program is probably one of the simplest, least expensive change drivers to deploy with minimum or no disruption to the system using existing basic quality tools and resources. With management support, proper training and motivation of existing workforce, and a *'start-up kit model'* on going beyond sustainability, a multi-functional team can easily deploy this initiative with a high possibility of success. Always keep in mind that this initiative can only occur if the system has reached the maturity level above basic compliance; otherwise, the first focus should be compliance as this element should be the benchmark of any system. Compliance is the first stepping stone to success. Without compliance, there is no consistent measurement of initiatives to promote growth and progress.

The author's book, *Auditing Beyond Compliance—Using a Portable System*, provides tools and strategies to help companies achieve the beyond-compliance level before pursuing beyond the sustainability level (see Figure 15.2).

The implementation of a lean-based continuous improvement program to generate additional savings is one path to achieve the level beyond compliance and beyond sustainability. How does a company achieve this level? Is it through the implementation of special improvement projects?

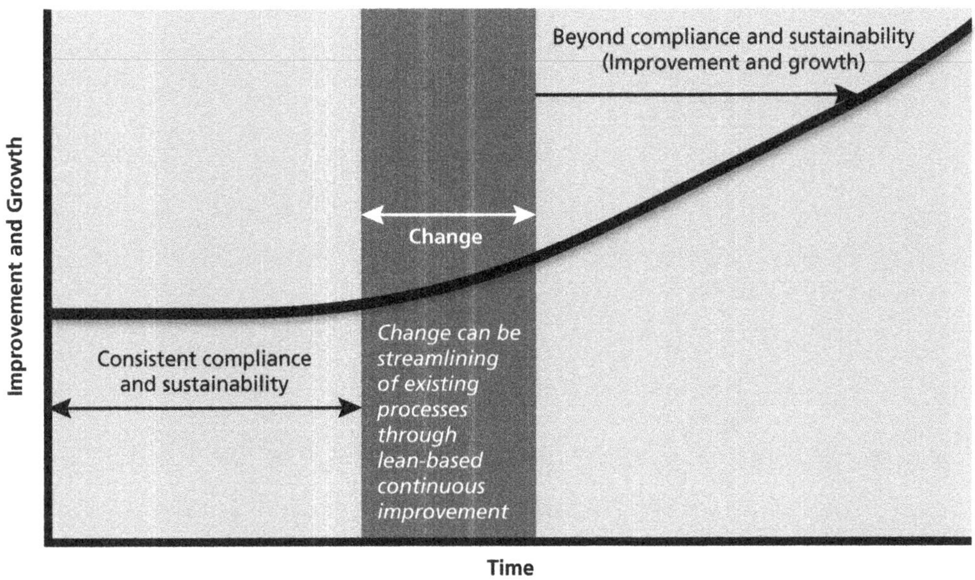

Figure 15.2 Path beyond compliance and beyond sustainability.

It does not work quite that way, although a special project to achieve this level is not an impossibility. The goal of this publication is to help you optimize programs or initiatives already in the system and performed day-to-day by the process owners. The only difference is the method of analyzing these process elements to convert 'old stuff' to 'new stuff.' What does this mean?

- Traditional methods such as root cause analysis as problem solving tool may be transformed into an improvement or savings tool by merely changing the style of data mining and application of information.
- The policing method of auditing may be transformed into an improvement partnership with operations and still retain independence of the audit. The traditional method of reporting audit findings may be transformed into improvement opportunities and savings, rather than a punitive implication.

- Verification of action item completion may be converted into a more dynamic indicator of effectiveness through the replacement of 'subjective' conclusions with measurable deliverables.

These are just the few day-to-day initiatives that can be polished to highlight the added value of existing stuff such as internal audits, root cause analysis, and verification of action plans. Nothing is new, except for the method of thinking and implementation.

16
Changes and Realignment with the Vision

Change is not an unusual element and could occur at any given time prompted by various causes. Change may occur due to customer requirements, market trends, regulatory ordinance, financial constraints, or other reasons that may impact the operational strategy in place. The design of a robust change management system will allow flexibility of any strategy model to accommodate changes during deployment and still maintain alignment with the vision.

Change has different levels of severity and sometimes can be subtle but with significant impact to the system; some changes can be incremental in nature and not noticeable until over a period of time when serious 'damage done' is manifested in various forms such as rejects, poor process performance, customer complaints, high claims rate, product returns, or other negative results.

Change management design should be integrated with the strategic plan and operational deployment to create a strong foundation for the accomplishment of the vision. A rigid strategic plan will create roadblocks and ineffective utilization of valuable resources. How? As an example, an inflexible system will serve as a barrier for the process owners to perform day-to-day tasks; at some point, such rigid systems will be circumvented through the creation of sub-systems to *bypass* the roadblock, giving rise to "hidden factories." This situation may be avoided by providing a system to process changes effectively and prevent the sub-optimization of resources. Will the creation of change management cause the drifting of the initial strategies away from the vision? The impact of an effective change management may actually strengthen the alignment of the strategies with the vision; the constant monitoring and adjustment of the system is similar to a driver in a traffic zone, checking the rear and side mirrors to ensure alignment of the vehicle with the traffic flow, with the goal of reaching the destination in a safe and timely manner. During this journey, some unexpected scenarios may occur, and a good driver will likely choose a logical option based on "lessons learned" from past experiences. If there is a roadblock, the best detour path is selected based on the options available (Figure 16.1).

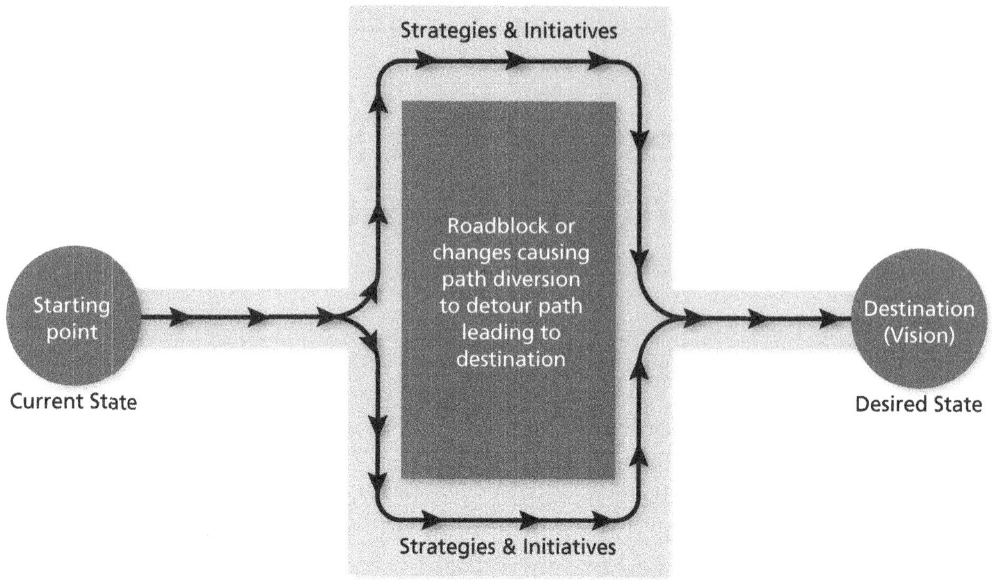

Figure 16.1 Changes and realignment of flexible strategies and initiatives.

Strategic planning should be flexible to allow changes, or mitigate and resolve roadblocks, and should have the elasticity to re-align the initiatives with the vision. In business, a similar concept applies; the soundness of the strategic plan depends on the business intelligence behind the plan providing a solid foundation and robust deployment of the initiatives to reach the goal despite changes that may impact the vision. What is business intelligence? Business intelligence, for this chapter's purpose, is defined simply as the extra energy exerted to achieve the business goal. Development and application of the needed business intelligence will serve as the guiding light to find the best path back to the main streamline—that is, the re-alignment of strategies and initiatives with the vision after a diversion (change).

Business intelligence may include:

- Marketing research to know the competition's weakness and use that as a driving force as company differentiator during the creation of vision or strategies.
- Defining internal weak spots as focal areas to prioritize and initiate improvement programs aligned with the vision and strategy.

  Example: If there are five processes available for the deployment of an improvement initiative, it may be beneficial to consider process performance as one indicator for selection. As the saying goes, "A chain is only as strong as its weakest link."

- Defining a special niche to capture the untapped zone. This concept is not limited to outside customers; it can be applicable to internal processes such as the development of non-traditional programs to achieve the goal.

  Example: Quality partnership with Operations on process streamlining to increase efficiency, minimize error, and provide savings. This is a transformation of the typical audit police role into quality partnership with the system to achieve level beyond compliance.
- Recognition of the workforce as an integral asset of the company, regardless of hierarchy.
- Conversion of roadblocks into challenges and opportunities for improvement and savings benefiting all stakeholders.

Example 16.1 Alignment of initiatives with market trend.

A California-based intraocular lens manufacturing company's vision was to capture more than 50% of the U.S. intraocular lens market in the next two years. Strategies included shorter order lead time through process streamlining and the development of an in-house laboratory staffed by highly qualified technical experts in the field. Before the initiatives could be completed, a sudden market change occurred. A foreign company entered the U.S. market and introduced the same quality lenses at a cheaper price and shorter lead time, thus saturating the intraocular lens market. What did the company do to survive this influx of competition? The company merged with a Swedish company manufacturing a unique patented accessory used during the implantation of the intraocular lens. This put the company and the business partner in a niche that survived the competition and gained a large percentage of the market share. This success story is an example of a flexible strategy that reacted quickly to the environmental changes using business intelligence.

Lesson Learned:

The success story in this example, just like any other success, will not last forever; continuous monitoring of internal indicators through the audit system and process metrics should provide feedback to the system to ensure that the initiatives are still effective in achieving the vision. The process metrics (sales, revenue growth, returns, etc.) will give the ultimate results needed by the stakeholders in making the appropriate move to ensure growth and stability of the system.

17

How Do You Promote Sustainability of an Initiative to the Grassroots Level?

Without management support and grassroots level buy-in, the sustainability of an operational initiative will not last (see Figure 17.1).

The first barrier to break down is the lack of understanding about the initiative's added value to the system and to personal growth and development. The fear of the unknown is a mindset that is difficult to combat as it is invisible and varies in intensity.

Figure 17.1 Sustainablity elements to maintain grassroots performance and growth.

Prepare the grassroots workers for the journey (inspire buy-in):

- Relay clear information and commitment to provide support to the workforce. This will help replace uncertainty with confident realization of the program's value. This is the first step to creating workforce buy-in. Once the idea is embraced, the workforce will be engaged in the development of pertinent metrics and will offer lesser resistance. Otherwise, the fear of the unknown sets in the mindset and may stay there if not mitigated at an early stage.
- Clarify management expectations. This is critical in aligning the efforts and initiatives to achieve the desired output. Success of this element increases the probability of an effective program.
- Establish the program flow and boundaries (example: explain the concept of DMAIC methodology).
- Instill importance of stakeholder interest, which includes the workforce interest (not sub-optimization to achieve a one-sided goal).
- Provide opportunities to contribute ideas; allow flexibility to think out of the box; avoid being rigid for the sake of self-inflicted compliance.
- Invest in training programs to enhance the workforce and create a motivating environment to optimize the workers' talent and skills.
- Encourage team effort (not monopoly). Participation in team initiatives builds cooperation and cross-functional exchange of knowledge and expertise to reach the mutual goal.
- Provide guidelines to the continuous improvement path and encourage input to promote buy-in.
- Provide communication tools (bulletin boards, stand-up/brief meetings for quick updates). Free information flow (rather than silos) advocates commitment to keep all levels of the organization notified of progress or changes.
- Create a two-way communication flow to discourage silos.
- Promote fairness and standard implementation of policies. Reward (or recognize) expected behavior and address unacceptable ones. Fairness and recognition come in different shapes and forms visible to the grassroots level—be consistent.

  Example: Errors due to inadvertent deviation should be addressed differently from repeating non-compliance with blatant disregard of rules.
- Nurture the workforce; the workers control the day-to-day quality of output. Knowledgeable and motivated employees are assets to the company. Treat both internal and external customers the way you want to be treated. The way management treats customers 'behind closed doors' is what the workers see. Set good examples.

- Run pilot runs to give 'hands-on' experience before the kick off. Roadblocks are sometimes not visible until encountered by the subject experts; optimize the grassroots level's expertise and feedback.

Involving the process owners as partners in this program empowers the process owners and creates built-in accountability and ownership at the core level.

Once grassroots core motivating elements are in place, a program's effectiveness may be measured or reflected in the following:

- Attendance or absenteeism
- Compliance to regulations and policies
- Success rate or decrease in repeating error rate
- Consistency of quality of work
- Feedback from peers or superiors
- Willingness to go the extra mile on a consistent basis when there is an urgent need, without being asked (versus running out the door at the end of day)
- Team cooperation
- Feedback from the employees
- Contribution to the company (e.g., improvement projects, savings, etc.)

These are just few examples, depending on the business structure; there may be company-specific criteria to measure employee performance and motivation. Some of these metrics are subjective; thus, consideration must be taken to ensure expectations are realistic and unbiased.

18

Integration of Strategic Planning, Risk Mitigation, Process Metrics, and Auditing

CHALLENGE RUN

The ultimate test of lessons learned is the use of the Challenge Run Kit discussed in the following pages. The Challenge Run Kit shows the step-by-step use of the models and tools discussed in this book in the integration of your company or departmental strategic planning, risk mitigation, development of process metrics, and verification of effectiveness through auditing.

For the challenge run (or trial run), choose a simple process. Depending on the scope of the selected process, the team may comprise the sole process owner only or a cross-functional team with subject expertise on the process.

For this trial run it is assumed that there is already an existing vision and strategy within the company; if none exist at this time, consider this project a continuous improvement initiative. It will be beneficial if the team members selected read this book prior to the pilot run.

A typical timeline based on a simple process with two to three cross-functional team members is approximately two to three months with measurable results. Other subject experts may be included to solicit input in addition to the selected team members. This timeline will vary depending on the process selection and schedule availability of the team to complete the core tasks described in the Challenge Run Starter Kit on the following pages.

CHALLENGE RUN STARTER KIT

Table 18.1 Challenge Run roadmap and recommended timeline.

Challenge Run – Core Steps	Week 1	Week 2	Week 3	Week 4	Week 5	Week 6	Week 7	Week 8–9	Week 10–14
1. Select a process for developing initiatives									
2. Hold preliminary brainstorming with potential cross-functional team for this project before drafting project charter	→								
3. Draft a project charter	→								
4. Present this plan to management for approval and support		→							
5. Team members to read this book to understand models		→	→	→					
6. Customize and hold workshops (1–4) with selected subject experts to solicit input for this project					→	→			
7. Summarize the input and recommendations solicited from the workshop participants for management review							→	→	
8. Perform any follow-up workshops if necessary to further identify the performance metrics on the actions approved by Manager of process understudy									→
9. Select top initiative and recommended action and metric solicited from the workshop. Keep in mind this is a trial run, therefore, it is best to choose the initiative that can be completed within the scrope of the project timeline. Once selected, review the process owners/ manager for any input and approval. Based on the input, adjust as needed. Finalize documentation requirements such as record forms, brief procedure on the process and training of the data collector. Refer to the templates in this book as needed.									→
10. Implement and follow-up effectiveness of the actions (results versus goal), adjust as needed. Follow-up should include a structured audit and review of results.									→

Table 18.2 Challenge Run checklist.

Task on Timeline	Additional Guidelines and Recommended Templates	Responsibility/ Status
1. Select process for this project.	**Template 14.6** – SIPOC Worksheet or **Template 14.3** – Brainstorming to identify the input and output of the selected process. This will help identify the gap if the desired output is not being met using the existing input.	
2. Hold brainstorming session with potential team before drafting the project charter.	**Template 14.3** – Brainstorming **Template 14.10** – Process Waste Walk may also be used prior to drafting the charter to identify any additional improvement opportunity not detected during the brainstorming. **Template 14.11** – Risk Assessment may also be used to help identify the focus points.	
3. Draft Project Charter using information solicited from item 2 above.	**Template 14.12** – Project Charter	
4. Present plan to management for approval.	Present Project Charter and adjust information as needed.	
5. Team members to read this book and review workshops.	Team should discuss any clarifications needed before project kick-off. Designate workshop facilitator; customize workshop to selected process.	
6. Customize and hold workshops 1-4.	Other subject experts may be invited in the workshop to solicit input on the process under evaluation.	
7. Summarize input and recommendations from the workshops.	**Template 14.8** – Identification of roadblocks or bottlenecks	
8. Perform any follow up workshops as needed to identify performance metrics.	**Template 14.9** – Data collection for process metrics	
9. Select top initiative.	In the selection of any initiative, associated roadblocks need to be identified to ensure countermeasures are put in place. Use Pareto analysis discussed in workshop.	
10. Implement the initiative and follow up within the designated timeline.	**Template 14.4** – Management Review – Initiative – Scorecard of Performance Metrics **Template 14.10** – Process Waste Walk may also be used during follow up to identify additional improvement opportunity.	

PART VI
Templates
Basic Quality and Lean Tools

Template 14.3

BRAINSTORMING WORKSHEET
DEPARTMENTAL OR PROCESS INITIATIVES

(to Support Vision and Strategy)

Purpose of this worksheet:
This is to document initiative ideas within the department or process to support the company vision and strategies. This form is applicable only if the vision and strategies have been defined by the company. The vision and the applicable strategies (if there are multiple, use one worksheet per strategy) should be listed by the department leader. Input from the team may be recorded individually by the members in section C for discussion.
The intent of this worksheet is to record ideas for further selection by the team. Details may be reviewed for feasibility during the discussion or may be attached to this worksheet.

A. Vision statement:

B. Brief description of strategy:

Metric to measure strategy's success?
(Note: This element will provide connectivity to the development of departmental initiatives in item C below).

C. Initiatives supporting item A and B above:

Brief description of proposed initiative (list possible roadblocks):	Estimated resource, technology support required, and timeline	Proposed performance metrics (benchmark and/goal) to measure progress of initiative

Submitted by: ______________________________ Date: ____________________

Template 14.4

MANAGEMENT REVIEW
Initiatives – Scorecard of Performance Metrics

Review Period: _______to_________
Completed by:__________________

Purpose of this form:

This form is to provide condensed status of the departmental initiatives to support the business strategies to achieve the vision. The core initiatives are the primary initiatives selected by the departmental leaders and approved by management as aligned with the vision/strategy.

Details of the individual initiatives may be provided by pertinent department leader.

Department	**Core Initiatives**	**Metric**	**Current Status**	**Goal**	**In track?** (if not, state plan)
Example: QA	*Initiative # QA1:* *Streamline process XX in 3 months by simplifying the procedures and reducing waste*	*Savings in labor cycle time waste reduction*	*Xx*	*a. Savings of $10K/mo.* *b. Reduction of process related error by 30%*	

Template 14.5

INTERNAL AUDIT CHECKLIST – Process Metrics

The purpose of this checklist is to structure the review of core performance metrics selected by the department and to provide feedback to the system. This checklist is not all encompassing, and should be used as addendum to the existing internal audit checklist. The questions may be asked at any sequence as deemed logical for the activity. Additional sheet may be used to attach results or comments. If root cause is needed, existing Corrective Action Plan form may be used.

Internal auditors(s):	
Date of audit:	
Process to be audited:	
Metrics to be audited in this process:	

	Checklist	Comments
	1. **Ask process owner to name the top* metrics being monitored for this process.** ***Note:** Top metrics depend on the process; typical 3-5 metrics Example: rework, reject, cycle time, on-time delivery	
	2. Are there goals set for each top metric? ___Yes ___No If yes, are the goals selected and approved by designated authorized personnel? If no, ask for the reason and how the process owners know acceptance criteria?	
	3. Review the collection history* to determine data pattern or behavior and ask process owner to explain the goal and the meaning of the behavior displayed by data. Some patterns that may impact goal and may require further root cause analysis are: __Negative trend __Constant value; none or insignificant fluctuation __Gaps of collection (missing data) __Excessive fluctuation from goal from period-to-period __Other patterns that may impact the goal ***Note:** History period will depend upon the available data or the frequency of collection. For example, for daily collection, a month's period may be sufficient to determine trend. Scope of review will be at the discretion of the auditor based on the situation.	
	4. Is there a review process of these top metrics? If any of the patterns occurred in the past, did it trigger any root cause analysis or action plan to mitigate the issue?	
	5. Do the process owners know why these metrics are selected? Ask process owners to explain reason.	
	6. **Is there a procedure governing this data collection that includes: frequency, process owner, review process, escalation process?** Is this process fully understood by the process owners (assess via interview or observation).	
	7. Prepare and list other pertinent questions prior to audit.	

Template 14.6

SIPOC WORKSHEET

Supplier-Input-Process-Output-Customer

Purpose of this form:

This simplified SIPOC form is to aid in identifying the **input** variables that become part of the **process** under evaluation or have an influencing effect or direct impact on the desired or expected **output**. This is a simplified SIPOC meant as a quick aid in identifying the vital few. Once the vital few are chosen, an in-depth root cause analysis may begin focusing on these critical items.
NOTE:
It is not uncommon to discover another critical element not initially recognized during this initial SIPOC study; analysis should be flexible to address new discoveries during the data mining.

This record may be discarded or made part of the quality records.

Prepared by :______________________________Date:______________

Reference #: ______________________________

CONDENSED SIPOC FORMAT

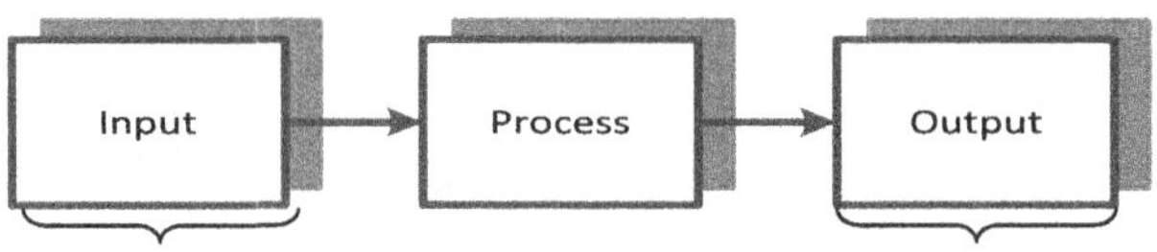

Input: List variables that have impact on the desired output: *Example: Training of operators* ☐ __________ ☐ __________ ☐ __________ ☐ __________	**Brief Description of the Process:**	**Output:** List Desired or Expected Output: *Example: Zero error on material traceability* ☐ __________ ☐ __________ ☐ __________ ☐ __________

Template 14.7

5-WHY – Root Cause Analysis Worksheet

Problem Reported by:	**Date:**
Reference Complaint Number:	

Problem Statement:

	What success factor was missing? (What could have prevented the situation?)	**Action or Performance metrics** that could have detected occurrence described under each **Why:**
Why 1: Why did the problem happen?		
Why 2: Why did Why 1 happen?		
Why 3: Why did Why 2 happen?		
Why 4: Why did Why 3 happen?		
Why 5: Why did Why 4 happen?		

Concluded root cause? **Action Plan?**

Template 14.8

Identification of Roadblocks or Bottlenecks

(based on simplified Force-Field Diagram Concept)

Purpose of this template:
The purpose of this procedure is to provide simple guidelines in identifying roadblocks or bottlenecks and assist in the root cause analysis or prioritization and development of initiatives or action plans.

Step 1. This format can be put on a board or flipchart and meeting members can start writing their input on the appropriate column.
Note: If there are several meeting members and members do not wish to make their comments in public, the members can write their comments on sticky pad. Give the members a few minutes to write their comments (such as: how can the issue or initiative be accomplished or what is blocking the completion of the initiative?)
Step 3: The meeting facilitator collects the notes and reads each one out loud before posting each note on the appropriate column (Column A or C).
Step 4: The meeting facilitator summarizes the results for review (may be escalated to the next level of decision makers).

A. **In favor** (what can be done to accomplish column B)	B. **Describe issue or initiative under evaluation**	C. **Against** (what is preventing accomplishment of column B)

Template 14.9

DATA COLLECTION FOR PROCESS METRICS

Purpose of this template:
This document is to provide guidelines in standardizing the responsibility, method of data collection, frequency, and any other pertinent information that may impact the data integrity. This is in lieu of verbal instruction to the data collector. Examples may be attached to this document to serve as template to the data collector, as applicable.

Process or department being monitored: ______________________
Start date: ______________ **End date:*** ______________________
**If task is continuous, put N/A on end date.*

Criteria:		
Process metrics being monitored:	*e.g., Scrap rate*	
Frequency of data collection:	*e.g., Every batch processed*	
Data to be collected:	*e.g., Total rejected units per batch for process XX, 3 shifts*	
Responsibility of data collection:	*e.g., Primary – Final inspector back up; in-process inspector*	
Source of data:	*e.g., Final inspection log – end of day/ daily report*	
Method of collection:	*e.g., Update of Excel log – Filename location xx, formula already embedded in the database*	
Method of submission for review:	*e.g., Submit weekly to the Director of Quality for review*	
Other instructions:		

Template 14.10

PROCESS WASTE WALK

Purpose of this checklist:

This checklist provides guidelines for identifying process wastes during a Process Waste Walk of any department or process. The Walk can be performed by the department designee at a selected frequency.

Instruction:

List wastes uncovered under each applicable category. Submit list to a review team (or department head) for review and initiation of applicable action plans (column D). If review team or departmental management decides that certain 'wastes' cannot be addressed for various reasons, put 'Not a Priority" for that item (column D).

Examples or pictures may be attached to this document to help the review.

Process Waste Walk Performed at: ____________________by:____________________

Start Date: _________________________Frequency of this initiative: ________________

A. Category of Waste	B. Examples	C. List of Actual Observations	D. Recommended Actions & Measurement of Potential Saving
Transportation	*Excessive walking, excessive movement of material, etc.*		
Inventory	*Excessive material or overstocking of non-priority material, etc.*		
Material	*Material wasted (over packaging, obsolescence of materials due to lack of first-in-first-out policy, etc.)*		
Waiting Time	*Delays during hand-off of processes*		
Over Processing	*Redundant inspections or recordings of same items, etc.*		
Over Production	*Poor planning not matching demand, etc.*		
Defects	*Rejects due to non-standard process, lack of training, etc.*		
Sub Optimization	*Poor resource planning due to volume fluctuation, use of supervision hours to fill in for workers, etc.*		

Template 14.11

RISK ASSESSMENT

Purpose of this template:

There are many ways to record risk assessment of an issue. The template below is a recommended format as it clearly shows the key elements to help make a decision on the mitigation choice. This template may be used by an individual or as a brainstorming record for a team designated to perform the risk assessment.

An example of a completed template below shows the simplicity and power of this form.

A. STAKEHOLDER EXPECTATION OR ISSUE	B. ROADBLOCK and RISK ASSESSMENT	C. ANTICIPATED IMPACT or FAILURE MODE	D. POSSIBLE RISK MITIGATION

(Arrows signify Opposing forces)

Risk Assessment:
Management need to evaluate the lesser risk between columns A and B, factoring quantifiable elements and customer goodwill.

Instructions on how to use the template:

1. **Column A:** List the stakeholder expectation or issue that is the topic for evaluation. This may be triggered by a customer complaint or internal process feedback for continuous improvement. This is similar to a root cause analysis performed using tools such as 5-whys. The focus in using this template is the highlight on the impact of the issue to help the decision makers in choosing the most cost efficient and effective path to risk mitigation.

2. **Column B: List the corresponding roadblocks and risk assessments.**

   Roadblock: Once the expectation on column A is listed, the evaluation team can begin to list the primary roadblocks preventing achievement of the expectation (i.e., reflected by the opposing arrow at the bottom of columns A & B, also known as 'force field').
   Risk Assessment: For each roadblock listed, the evaluation team should list the risk associated with the roadblock.

3. **Column C**: List the anticipated impact or anticipated failure mode due to the roadblocks if not addressed or mitigated.
4. **Column D:** List the possible mitigation and associated costs.

Example - RISK ASSESSMENT LEAN TOOL

A. STAKEHOLDER EXPECTATION	B. ROADBLOCK and RISK ASSESSMENT	C. ANTICIPATED IMPACT or FAILURE MODE	D. POSSIBLE RISK MITIGATION
Customers expects that the Customer portal tracing for open orders will be operational by 3rd quarter of this year as part of the account contract.	**Roadblock:** Portal is showing minor inconsistencies, about 99% accuracy, troubleshooting will not be completed by the target date. **Risk assessment:** New customer may be aggravated to discover inaccurate information (even if it is minor) if released before validation. Decision needed which is riskier: release portal at 99% accuracy or delay release until accuracy (unknown completion date) is 100%?	If customer uses the slightly inaccurate portal, there will be potential complaints at these costs: · Potential customer complaints, approx. XX/week (each complaint cost approx. XX to process) · Mitigation of customer complaints will use Customer Service and support resources, approx. XX/week · Potential customer dissatisfaction may affect future opportunities of XX% revenue contribution	· Outsource validation of portal to expedite completion, cost XX · Offer cost XX% reduction to compensate for delayed release of portal · Release 'as is' with containment plan (e.g. temporary additional resource to manually check), cost XX, while continually working on improvement with timeline of XX.

Risk Assessment:
Management need to evaluate the lesser risk between columns A and B, factoring quantifiable elements and customer goodwill.

Template 14.12

PROJECT CHARTER No. ___

Purpose of this form: To document the life of the project.
Initiated by:_______________________ Date:_______________________
Approved by: _______________________ Date:_______________________

A. Problem Statement:
B. Scope of the Project:
C. Goal (benchmark versus desired output; initial discussion of metrics)
D. Team: Champion: Project leader: Team members/roles:
E. Data collection methodology:
F. Milestones/responsibility matrix/timeline:
G. Data analysis methodology (review of metrics):
H. Summary/conclusion /recommendations:
I. Approval of recommendations:
J. Verification of effectiveness (e.g., review of metrics' trend for a period of time)
K. Hand-off and implementation plan (to include documentation, training, structuring of metrics, etc.)
L. Approval of hand-off/project closure:

PART VII
Workshops on Basic Quality Lean Tools

WORKSHOP 1

Identification of Process Metrics for Internal Process

PURPOSE OF WORKSHOP: This workshop aims to give hands-on development of performance metrics. This workshop will help the process owners understand these concepts through actual application rather than theoretical explanation. There are many methods in the identification and development of performance metrics; this workshop is just one method.

ATTENDEES: Facilitator to lead the workshop (may be one of the process owners). Approximately 5 to 15 process owners.

ESTIMATED DURATION OF WORKSHOP: 1 hour

MATERIALS NEEDED: Sticky notes, flipchart or white board (room wall may be used to display sticky notes instead of flipchart or white board).

INSTRUCTIONS: Note—Above each step, the different phases of the DMAIC process are highlighted to help the participants identify the DMAIC phase for each step.

D	M	A	I	C

1. **DEFINE THE PROBLEM**

Before the workshop, facilitator and process owners must have already identified the process to be studied.

For this workshop, the process example under study is **IT support**. (See Figure W1.1)

2. **BRAINSTORMING**

Ask the participants to write on the sticky note the acceptable criteria for the process to be considered successful. Write one criteria per one sticky note.

D	**M**	A	I	C

3. **MEASURE THE DATA**

After the five-minute time limit, collect the sticky notes from the participants, shuffling them in random order.

4. **GROUP and CATEGORIZE DATA**

Facilitator will read each sticky note aloud and stick it onto the board.

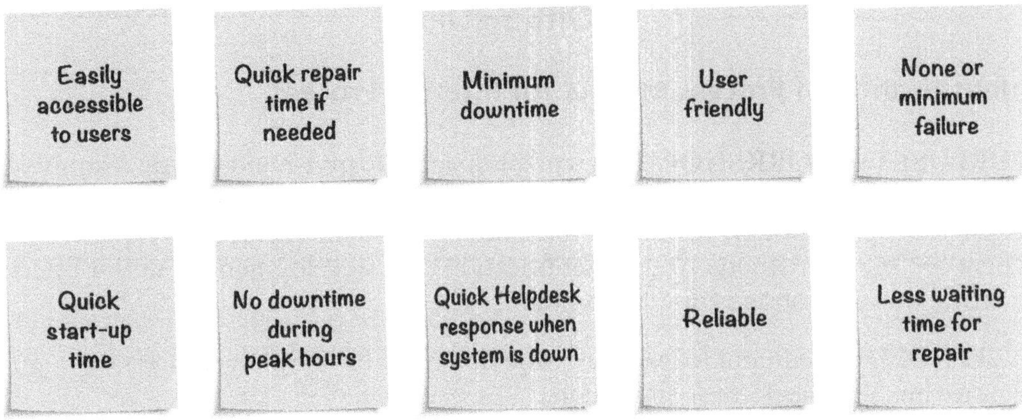

Figure W1.1 Examples of criteria for successful IT support.

D	M	**A**	I	C

5. ANALYZE DATA (Pareto analysis will be used for this workshop)

As the facilitator reads the sticky notes out loud, similar ones are grouped together. Input from the participants should be considered during the grouping of the notes. In some cases, the categories may have been worded differently, but alluding to the same concept. If this is the case, as needed, create a category name to represent all the sticky notes under that category (in Figure W1.2, Category 1 is named "Minimum Downtime or Failure" to represent all the similar notes put under this category).

After grouping the sticky notes, make a simple tally sheet for each category and choose the top three categories with the most sticky notes. This is Pareto analysis, or choosing of the vital few.

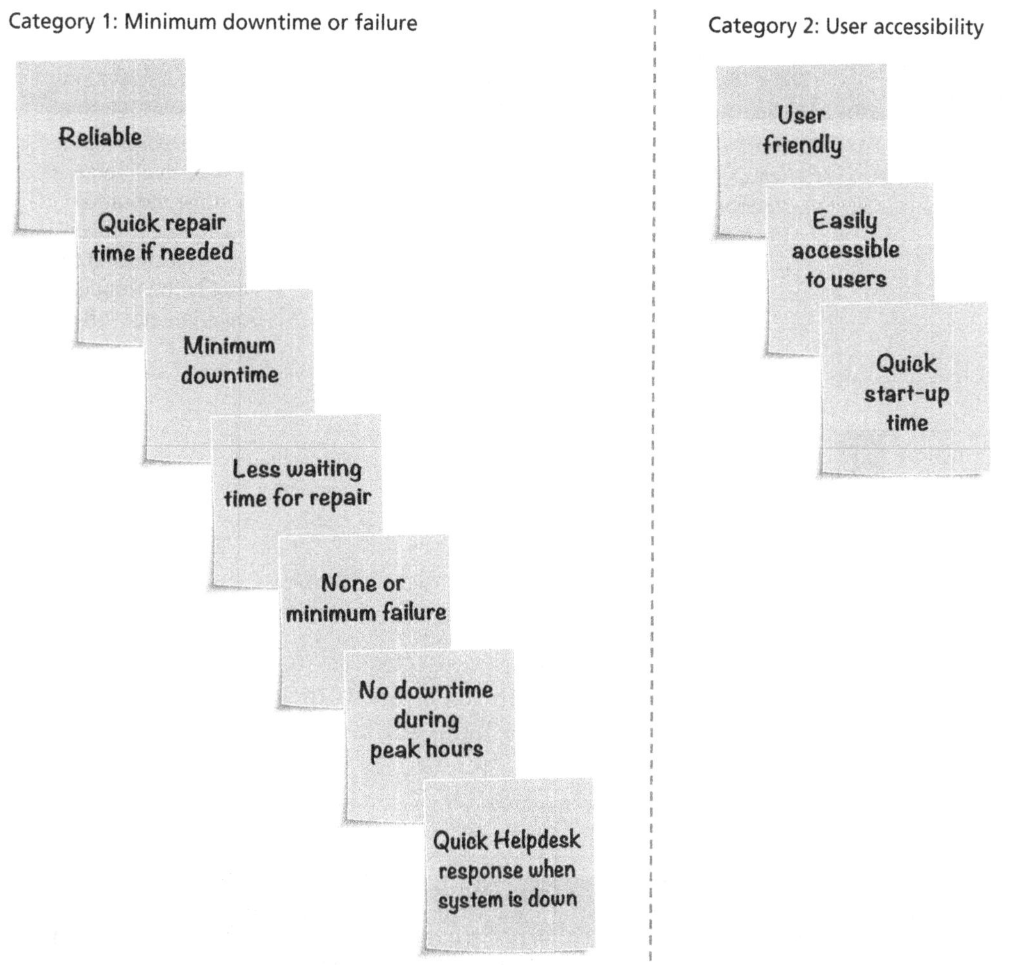

Figure W1.2 Categorized input from Figure W1.1.

6. BREAKDOWN OF DATA

Separate the participants into manageable groups for discussion for about 20 minutes. Ask each group to identify:

- Action(s) needed to address the criteria
- Roadblocks preventing the action to be completed
- Countermeasures to address roadblocks

The group may list the action(s) and roadblock(s) on sticky notes similar to method described in step 2 – Brainstorming. Final results may be recorded in format like Table W1.1.

Table W1.1 Final brainstorming results.

A. Criteria	B. Action needed to address the criteria	C. Roadblock preventing the action to be completed	D. Countermeasure to address roadblocks
Minimum downtime or failure.	There needs to be a simple, accurate, and standard system to track downtime per user.	Different software is in place and it is cumbersome to track the cumulative users' downtime per software.	User's helpdesk ticket for repair will require a simpler indication of software problem (e.g., defect code) to simplify the trending of downtime per software type.

D M A I C

7. IMPROVEMENT

Once the team agrees on the countermeasure actions, the performance metrics (i.e., measurement of success in meeting the criteria) need to be identified.

The group may take another 15 minutes discussion to identify the metrics. Step 2, Brainstorming, may be used to get this input from the group. Recording of the metrics may use the format similar to Table W1.2.

Table W1.2 Recorded metrics.

A. Criteria	B. Action needed to address the criteria	C. Roadblock preventing the action to be completed	D. Countermeasure to address roadblocks	E. Measure of success or performance metrics
Minimum downtime or failure	There needs to be a simple, accurate and standard system to track downtime per user.	Different software is in place and it is cumbersome to track the cumulative users' downtime.	Phase 1: A simple tracking of users' helpdesk ticket for repair will be developed including a coding system to easily identify software problem. This will facilitate trending of downtime per software type. Phase 2: This will allow in-depth review of root causes and target most problematic software with excessive downtime.	a. Failure rate per software type submitted via Helpdesk ticket. b. Downtime rate caused by each software type.

D | M | A | I | **C**

8. **CONTROL phase may be a separate follow-up workshop**

Control may be achieved after a validation period to ensure that the metrics in place are achievable.

Once the proposed metrics' trend is met, this improvement phase (goal needs to be set) can be controlled via monitoring of the chosen performance metric for this process. Controlling this process change to ensure consistent results and continuing effectiveness may include, but is not limited to, the following:

- Structured and periodic monitoring of the metric by the process owners so immediate feedback may be given to the system before a trend becomes irreversible.
- Inclusion of this metric in the internal audit program.
- Procedural documentation of the process to standardize method and provide training material for pertinent employees.

WORKSHOP 2

Application of the DMAIC flow, Force Field Diagram, and Pareto Analysis for Root Cause Analysis of Internal Process

PURPOSE OF WORKSHOP: This workshop aims to give hands-on application of lean tools *(Brainstorming method, Simplified Force Field Diagram, and Pareto concept)* using the DMAIC methodology. This workshop will help the process owners understand these concepts through actual application rather than theoretical explanation.

ATTENDEES: Facilitator to lead the workshop (may be one of the process owners). Approximately 5 to 10 process owners.

ESTIMATED DURATION OF WORKSHOP: 1 hour

MATERIALS NEEDED: Sticky notes, flipchart or white board (room wall may be used to display sticky notes instead of flipchart or white board).

INSTRUCTIONS: Note—Above each step, the different phases of the DMAIC process are highlighted to help the participants identify the DMAIC phase.

D M A I C

1. DEFINE THE PROBLEM

Before the workshop, facilitator and process owners must have already identified the problem to be studied.

Example: Receiving inspection's performance metric shows an average of 95% success rate of releasing acceptable parts to the assembly line. The requirement is 100% acceptable parts at any given time.

2. BRAINSTORMING

Ask the participants to write on the sticky note what they think are the root causes why Receiving inspection cannot achieve the 100% requirement. Write one root cause per one sticky note.

D M A I C

3. MEASURE THE DATA

After the five-minute time limit, collect the sticky notes from the participants, shuffling them in random order.

4. GROUP or CATEGORIZE DATA

Facilitator will read each sticky note aloud and stick it onto the board. As the facilitator reads the sticky note out loud, similar ones are group together. Input from the participants should be considered during the grouping of the notes. After grouping the sticky notes, make a simple tally sheet for each category and choose the top three categories with the most sticky notes. This is Pareto analysis, or choosing of the vital few.

D M A I C

5. ANALYZE DATA (Pareto analysis will be used for this workshop)

Choose the top three categories from step 4 above. In some cases, the categories may have been worded differently, but alluding to the same concept. If this is the case, as needed, create the category name to represent all the sticky notes under that category. Put the top three categories in separate sticky note and post on the board as shown in Figure W2.1.

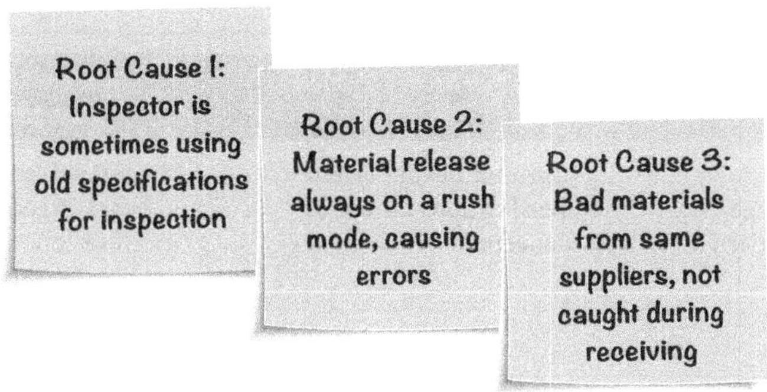

Figure W2.1 Top three possible root causes.

6. **BREAKDOWN OF DATA**

Separate the participants into three groups; assign one of the three root causes for each group to discuss for about 15-20 minutes.

Each group should list at leastone reason why the root cause assigned to the group occurs and how this can be corrected (list the roadblocks). This concept is sometimes called a force field diagram (opposing forces blocking the success of an action). The group may list their reason and roadblocks on sticky notes similar to Figure W2.2 or the group can use a matrix similar to Table W2.1.

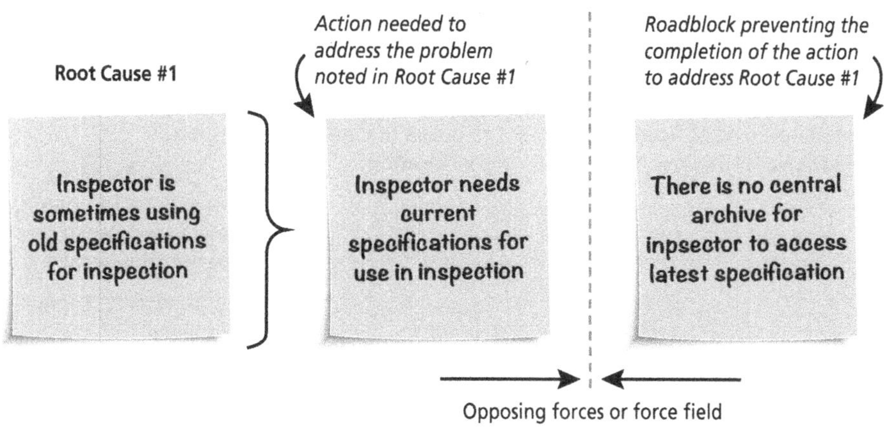

Figure W2.2 Force field concept using sticky notes.

Table W2.1 Force field concept using a matrix.

Root cause	Action needed to address the problem	Roadblock preventing the action to be completed
Root cause 1: Inspector is sometimes using old specifications for inspection.	Inspector needs current specifications for use in inspection.	There is no central archive for inspector to access the latest specification.
Root cause #2	Xxx	Xxx
Root cause #3	Xxx	Xxx

D	M	A	I	C

7. DEPLOYMENT (IMPROVEMENT & CONTROL)

Once the team agrees on the actions to be taken (column D) resulting from the discussion above, the next step is the actual deployment of the actions with assigned process owners and timeline (Table W2.2).

Table W2.2 Action plan to counteract the roadblocks.

A. Root cause	B. Action needed to address the problem	C. Roadblock preventing the action to be completed	D. Action plan to address roadblocks responsibilities & timeline
Root cause 1: Inspector is sometimes using old specifications for inspection.	Inspector needs current specifications for use in inspection.	There is no central archive for inspector to access the latest specification.	a. Create central specification archive accessible to inspector. b. Update Receiving inspection procedure cross-referencing use of central specification archive. Responsibility: Engineering Manager Timeline: xxxx
Root cause #2	Xxx	Xxx	Xxx
Root cause # 3	Xxx	Xxx	Xxx

Improvement of the process may be monitored using the benchmark versus goal, normally indicated in the problem statement under the Define phase of the DMAIC flow.

- **Performance metric for this case may be the rate of releasing acceptable part-based on the input of the system**
- **Benchmark:** Current 95% success rate (noted in the problem statement above).
- **Goal:** 100% success rate of releasing acceptable parts

The team can choose a validation period to monitor the effectiveness of the selected action items. The length of the validation period is at the discretion of the process owners with consideration of the risk level, etc.

A simple matrix can be used to record the validation, for example, weekly measurement of the performance metric or a frequency matching the process owners' flow (Table W2.3).

Table W2.3 Simple matrix to record the validation.

Reference	Success rate–Week 1	Success rate–Week 2	Success rate–Week 3
Benchmark: 95% success rate Goal: 100%	Xxx	Xxx	Xxx

D | M | A | I | **C**

8. **CONTROL**

Once the desired trend is met, this improvement phase can be controlled via monitoring of the chosen performance metric for this process. Controlling this process change to ensure consistent results and continuing effectiveness may include, but is not limited to, the following:

- Structured and periodic monitoring of the metric by the process owners so immediate feedback may be given to the system before a trend becomes irreversible.
- Inclusion of this metric in the internal audit program.
- Procedural documentation of the process to standardize method and provide training material for pertinent employees.

WORKSHOP 3

Understanding and Application of the Fishbone Diagram for Root Cause Analysis of Internal Process

PURPOSE OF WORKSHOP: This workshop aims to give hands-on application of the fishbone diagram, a lean tool for analysis. This workshop will help the process owners understand these concepts through actual application rather than theoretical explanation.

ATTENDEES: Facilitator to lead the workshop (may be one of the process owners). Approximately 5 to 10 process owners.

ESTIMATED DURATION OF WORKSHOP: 1 hour

MATERIALS NEEDED: Sticky notes, flipchart or white board (room wall may be used to display sticky notes instead of flipchart or white board.

1. DISCUSS DEFINITION OF FISHBONE DIAGRAM

What is a fishbone diagram?

This is a visual display of the different cause-and-effect variables of a problem or situation. The typical influencing elements of the cause-and-effect variables are called 6Ms: Material, Manpower, Method, Measurements, Mother Nature (Environment), and Machines. Each of these variables has sub-elements, depending on the situation under study.

Draw a typical model of a fishbone diagram on the board, as shown in Figure W3.1.

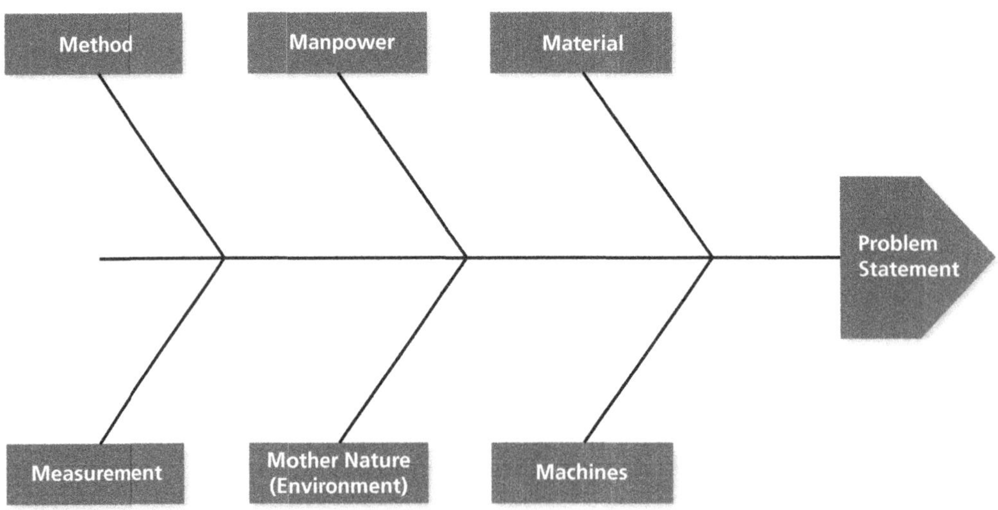

Figure W3.1 Typical fishbone diagram.

2. **DEFINE the Problem Statement**

The problem statement example for this workshop is a repeating non-compliance to procedures, causing decline in service performance (actual is 80% versus goal of 98%).

3. **BRAINSTORMING**

Give participants about five to ten minutes to write on a sticky note the possible causes of the problem statement, one cause per sticky note. Ask the participants to stick their sticky notes on the board. Possible results are shown in Figure W3.2.

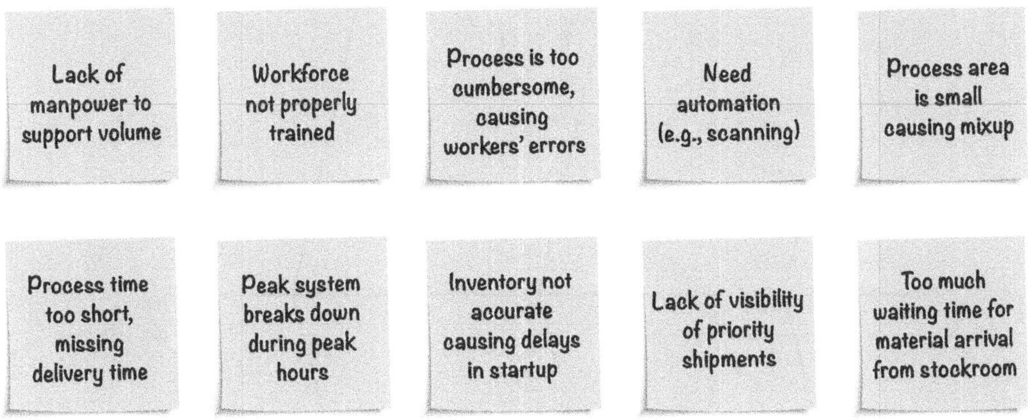

Figure W3.2 Possible causes.

4. **SORT DATA**

Ask volunteers put sticky notes under the most appropriate category as shown in Figure W3.3. Repeat this process until all the sticky notes are in the fishbone diagram.

5. **ANALYZE DATA**

Select the most critical items listed under each category and prioritize the items with the most risk or impact in the resolution of the problem statement. The team has to decide which items can be realistically addressed through prioritization and designing immediate and long-term action plans.

The fishbone diagram is a tool to make these influencing variables visible to the process owners and management; resolution of these issues may require escalation to the next hierarchy level in the company to ensure buy-in and accountability.

An example of action plan matrix to record the analysis resulting from the fishbone analysis is shown in Table W3.1.

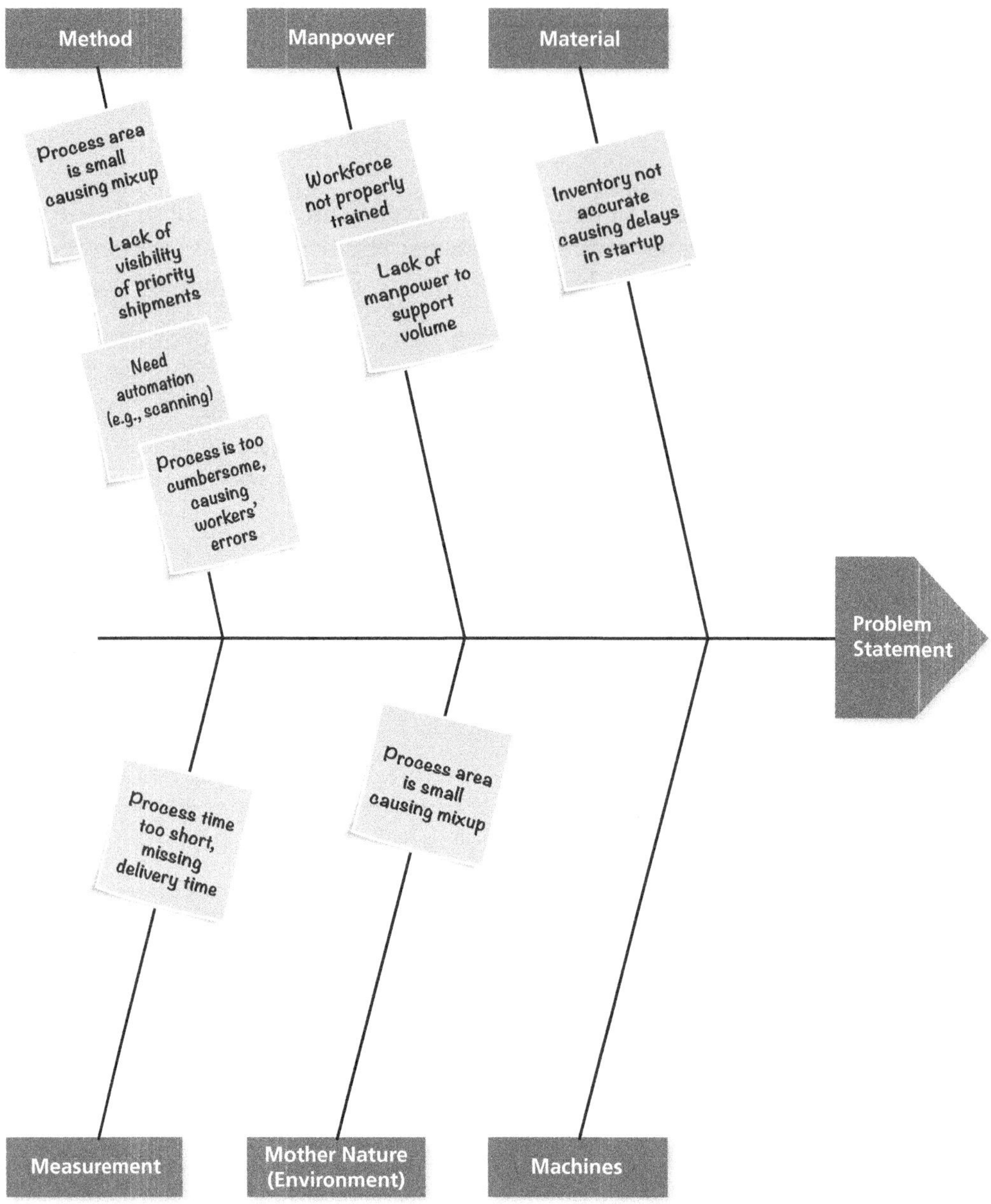

Figure W3.3 Possible causes categorized.

Table W3.1 Fishbone analysis action plan matrix.

Element of the Fishbone Diagram	Action Plan	Examples of Measure of Success (Performance Metrics)
Method		
Lack of visibility of priority shipments	Report of due dates will be made easily accessible to dock management for timely review.	On-time delivery trend before and after implementation of action plan.
Access area is small, causing mix up	Develop/implement 5S, assign process owner and frequency of auditing the area to ensure consistent compliance.	Develop 5S criteria and measure compliance on a set frequency.
Process is too cumbersome, causing worker errors and needing automation	Phase 1: Perform process walks and identify bottlenecks through observation and time study. Phase 2: Review results of Phase 1 and involve process owners in the identification of improvement opportunities for process-owners' controlled variables as well system's gap for escalation to management.	Time study before and after Phase 2, against goal (to be set). Error rate before and after Phase 2, against goal (to be set). Process performance (benchmark: 80% versus goal of 98%).
Manpower	Xx	Xx
Material	Xx	Xx
Measurement	Xx	Xx
Mother Nature (Environment)	Xx	Xx
Machines	Xx	Xx

WORKSHOP 4

Streamlining Processes through the Identification and Reduction of Waste

PURPOSE OF WORKSHOP: This workshop aims to give hands-on understanding of process wastes and how they can be reduced or eliminated to maximize resources as well as trigger savings. This workshop will help the process owners understand the different forms of process waste through actual application rather than theoretical explanation.

ATTENDEES: Facilitator to lead the workshop (may be one of the process owners). Approximately 5 to 10 process owners.

ESTIMATED DURATION OF WORKSHOP: 1 hour

MATERIALS NEEDED: Sticky notes, flipchart or white board (room wall may be used to display sticky notes instead of flipchart or white board).

1. **DISCUSSION ON THE DIFFERENT FORMS OF PROCESS WASTE**

Facilitator to discuss the types of wastes and examples given in Table W4.1 as introduction of the waste reduction initiative.

Process streamlining does not necessarily involve capital expense; the streamlining may be the simple identification and reduction of wastes to enhance process efficiency and lesson errors or variations. There are many types of wastes, as shown in the list of common wastes below; the simplest types are the ones that can be controlled by the process owners.

Table W4.1 Typical defect categories (wastes).

A. Typical Defect Categories	B. Examples
Transportation	Excessive walking, excessive transfer of materials/resource
Inventory	Excessive inventory
Motion	Excessive bending, lifting, twisting
Waiting	Waiting time for materials, system downtime
Over-Processing	Redundant handling or inspection
Over-Production	Wasted resource allocated to process non-priority items stored in warehouse
Defect	Lack of workforce training causing defects, lack of proper tools to prevent defects, non-standard process causing fluctuating quality
Sub-optimization	Not optimizing resources (e.g. supervisors working in assembly line due to poor resource allocation)

Reference: http://www.isixsigma.com/dictionary/8-wastes-of-lean/

2. BRAINSTORMING

After the orientation on the types of wastes described in step 1 above, give participants about five to ten minutes to write on a sticky note the possible wastes they can identify in their areas. Ask the participants to write one form of waste per sticky note. Notes that are similar may be combined, as appropriate.

At the end of the 10 minutes, ask the participants to stick their notes on the board for class discussion. Ask the author of each sticky note to briefly describe (about one to two minutes) the listed waste and ask the participants if they have added information. The purpose of this open discussion is to allow inputs from the other participants' perspective, not a point for argument or debate. Possible results are shown in Figure W4.1.

Figure W4.1 Waste examples.

3. GROUP BRAINSTORMING

Sort participants into groups of manageable size and divide the listed wastes for group discussion. Allow about 20 minutes for each group to discuss the assigned waste and identify possible root causes and recommended action to address root cause.

Each group may use a flipchart to record the results of the group discussion as shown in matrix below (Table W4.2).

Table W4.2 Group discussion matrix.

A. Wastes	B. Possible root cause	C. Recommended action to address root cause
Waiting time during first article inspection		

Assumption: For the purpose of this workshop, it will be assumed that the participants agreed that wastes in Figure W4.1 are controllable by the process owners and can be addressed without difficulty. It will also be assumed, for the purpose of discussion, that the root causes and actions recommended by the participants are applicable to this workshop study. In some cases, there may be a need to escalate the initiatives prior to implementation to ensure optimum use of resources.

4. GROUP PRESENTATION

At the end of the time allotted for group discussion, post each group's matrix for class discussion. Ask each group to present the waste assigned to the group including the root causes (column B) and recommended actions (column C). Allow approximately 10 minutes per group.

After each presentation, participants may be asked to recommend measures of success or performance metrics (column D).

Below is an example of the compiled group presentations and recommended metrics (Table W4.3). The proposed actions will require a timeline and responsible owners for these actions to produce measurable results.

Escalation of these actions into departmental projects is an option to increase the visibility of the initiative's progress.

Table W4.3 Compiled group presentations and recommended metrics.

A. Waste	B. Possible cause	C. Proposed action	D. Proposed metrics
Waiting time during first article inspection	The process needs to be reviewed to assign workers possible tasks while waiting for the first article inspection.	Workers will be given training on 5S and will perform 5S checklist during the waiting time.	Waiting time before and after action implementation.

A. Waste	B. Possible cause	C. Proposed action	D. Proposed metrics
Too much walking to retrieve materials	Lay out of the material retrieval process and material release point not optimized.	Review layout involving process owners' input to maximize efficiency of this process. Kanban system will also be evaluated. Kanban – a scheduling system to support lean on just-in-time production. *http://en.wikipedia.org/wiki/Kanban*	Cycle time before and after the action implementation.

Table W4.3 Compiled group presentations and recommended metrics *(continued).*

A. Waste	B. Possible cause	C. Proposed action	D. Proposed metrics
Redundant recording of inspection information	Records not easily accessible to all users (therefore, users, create their own recordkeeping).	Centralized data archive will be evaluated. Input from users will be obtained on the reason for repeat recording of data to further simplify the process.	Users' time saved before and after the action implementation.

A. Waste	B. Possible cause	C. Proposed action	D. Proposed metrics
Note: These notes are similar and can be grouped together. Overtime due to fluctuating production volume Errors due to fatigue-excessive overtime	Peak seasons require high resource support; critical processes have few trained personnel causing overtime when volume is high.	Perform a simple time study to identify peak hours and needed resource to identify gaps. Evaluate optimum staggering of resources and cross-training to increase flexibility and resource pool.	Overtime and error rate due to machine failure before and after the action implementation.

A. Waste	B. Possible cause	C. Proposed action	D. Proposed metrics
Supervisors not supervising – too busy doing rework	Process needs to be reviewed to identify reason for rework.	Perform process walk of the core steps and acceptance criteria versus customer requirements. A SIPOC diagram may be used.	Quantity/cost of rework before and after the action implementation.

Table W4.3 Compiled group presentations and recommended metrics *(continued).*

A. Waste	B. Possible cause	C. Proposed action	D. Proposed metrics
Obsolete parts wasting space	Machine preventive maintenance not done consistently. Production usage does not allow enough downtime to schedule regular maintenance.	Review production peak schedule and maintenance requirement to evaluate staggering of these critical schedules. The goal is to identify a window of time for regular maintenance.	Preventive maintenance compliance rate Scrap rate due to machine failure before and after the action implementation
Obsolete parts wasting space	Obsolete parts have accumulated throughout the years, occupying space.	A review team (e.g., Material Review Board) needs to provide a timeline to structure review and disposition of the obsolete parts.	Quantity and cost of inventory before and after the action implementation.

5. VERIFICATION OF EFFECTIVENESS

A follow-up workshop may be beneficial to follow up on the actions' progress and any roadblocks encountered by the process owners. This structured and measurable verification process will increase the accountability of the tasks' completion and results will provide an empowerment to the process owners.

Glossary

AS9100: Quality standard based on ISO 9001:2008, with additional elements pertaining to the aerospace industries.

Auditing Beyond Compliance: An auditing method focusing not only in compliance verification but also in continuous improvement partnership with Operations. The author has also written a book with this title, published by Quality Press.

backhoe wheelie: Vehicle maneuver in which the front wheel or wheels come off the ground due to sufficient torque being applied to the rear wheel or wheels *(Ref. https://en.wikipedia.org/wiki/Wheelie).*

Balanced Scorecard: A lean model focusing on the interrelationship of the typical business elements, financial aspect, internal process capabilities, manpower skill set, and customer satisfaction. Satisfaction of each of these elements in any business decision-making requires balancing the risk factors associated with each element to optimize opportunities and benefits.

benchmark: Point of reference; see also current state.

buy-in: Workforce's voluntary acceptance of a concept or change through the realization of benefits.

core processes: Critical processes significantly impact the overall success of the work flow. The identification of core processes may be based on, but not limited to, the following factors: risk, customer requirement, regulatory scope.

critical-to-quality (CTQ): Elements that have significant impact on the success of a process; in some cases, critical-to-quality is used interchangeably with success factor.

current state: Typically used as the benchmark for measuring the progress or effectiveness of an initiative in comparison with the goal.

cycle time: The time it takes to complete a process or task.

DMAIC: The acronym stands for define-measure-analyze-improve-control. This is a core concept in the implementation of Lean Six Sigma processes. This discipline aids in the in-depth analysis of an issue, problem, or opportunity through a systematic approach—identifying the problem, developing an effective data collection, applying basic tools to analyze the meaning of the collected data to trigger an improvement, and controlling the pertinent variables to sustain the changes or improvement.

8-D: The eight disciplines (8D) model is a problem solving approach, consisting of 8 pinciples: team formation, problem statement, interim containment, root cause analysis, permanent actions, validation of actions, preventive measure, congratulating the team for achievement.

first article inspection: Typically refers to the evaluation of the set up in a manufacturing process before mass production. First article inspection is normally done before the start of a shift or when there is a change in the process variables, such as change in material lot number, change of operator, change in material set-up, etc. This is to detect any possible anomaly before running the batch. First article inspection's complexity is dependent on the item under evaluation, ranging from visual inspection to chemical analysis, etc.

fishbone diagram: A lean tool for problem solving through the analysis of common process variables known as 6Ms (manpower, machine, measurement, method, manpower, Mother Nature, and material). These variables are depicted in a diagram to show the elements interrelationship.

5-Whys analysis: An evaluation tool using the technique of asking 'why' to drill down to the core root cause. The discovery of the root cause may take fewer or more than five 'why' questions, depending on the situation.

force field diagram: A lean tool used in evaluating the actions that will address the issue under evaluation with consideration to the opposing factors. This evaluation is typically represented by documenting these two factors side-by-side in two columns for visibility to the review team.

GMP: Acronym stands for good manufacturing practices, typically associated with medical devices. However, other non-medical industries also use this phrase to mean best practices.

grassroots level: Pertains to the process owners or workforce that has 'hands-on' responsibilities on the process.

hidden factory: A term that refers to deviations from the standard that are not visible to the organization. A hidden factory typically results in wastes and errors. There are many reasons for the existence of the hidden factory; in some cases, they are by-products of inefficiencies.

ISO: Acronym refers to International Organization for Standardization, a quality standard focusing on the management and improvement of the quality management system.

layered metrics: A breakdown of a core metric to identify variables impacting the core metric. For example, on-time delivery, a core metric, may be impacted by material availability and equipment reliability to manufacture on time and therefore ship on time. With this breakdown, focus may be concentrated on the weak layer causing the failure. In this example, if the manufacturing delays are frequently caused by machine breakdown, equipment downtime may be a useful layer metric to add in the evaluation of the on-time delivery performance.

Lean Six Sigma: A discipline and methodology for streamlining processes to reduce variation and waste.

moment of truth: A perception during the brief encounter or interaction. For example, a receptionist's warm greeting may make a lasting impression to the visiting customer.

outlier: In statistics, this is a value outside the range of other values.

Pareto analysis: The vital few elements that have primary impact on the situation being analyzed. Due to time and resource constraints, it is cost effective to define the vital few variables impacting the analysis.

PDCA: Acronym stands for Plan-Do-Check-Act.

productivity: A measure of work completed within a period of time by the resource performing the task. One common measure is handling units per hour. Handling units may pertain to number of pieces, weight, boxes, lot, etc.

quarantine: Segregation of suspect material until a resolution can be made.

Sequoia: The giant sequoia (Sequoiadendron giganteum) is the world's most massive tree, and the largest living organism on Earth.

silo: In lean culture, this typically means isolation or control of information flow to prevent access outside a select group. This is not a good practice as it obstructs visibility of data that may be critical for decision making.

SIPOC: Acronym stands for Supplier-Input-Process-Output-Customer. It is a lean tool for analyzing the incoming and outgoing variables of a process.

sub-optimization: A form of waste caused by not maximizing the potential capability or capacity available, for example assigning an engineer to perform physical inventory to minimize hiring additional hourly labor. The engineering talent is not being optimized in this case.

success factor: A critical element directly impacting the achievement of the process goal. The success factor is normally used to measure the performance level. For example, in transportation business, the core success factors are on-time delivery, accurate quantity, and intact products.

TL 9000: Quality standard based on ISO 9001:2008, with additional elements applicable to the telecommunication industries.

TS 16949: Quality standard based on ISO 9001:2008, with additional elements applicable to automotive industries.

waste: In the business world, this refers to any non-added value use of resources.

References

American National Standards Institute (ANSI), International Organization for Standardization (ISO), American Society for Quality (ASQ). ANSI/ISO/ASQ Q9001-2015. *Quality management systems – Requirements*

Bautista Smith, J., November 2015. "Analyzing Risk Through the Thales Shadow Concept," ASQ *Six Sigma Forum Magazine.*

Bautista Smith, J., July 30 and August 6, 2014. "Auditing Beyond Compliance – Discover Your Hidden Factory," workshops at Purdue University sponsored by Purdue TAP group, IN.

Bautista Smith, J., June 2014. "Increasing Business Efficiency," Continuing Education workshop sponsored by IUPUI Continuing Education, IN.

Bautista Smith, J., April 2013. "Can One Per Cent Rule?" ASQ *Lean Division Newsletter.*

Bautista Smith, J., July 2012. *Auditing Beyond Compliance – Using a Portable Universal Quality Lean Audit Model,* Quality Press 2012. http://asq.org/quality-press/display-item/index.html?item=H1430 http://www.amazon.com/Auditing-Beyond-Compliance-Portable-Universal/dp/0873898400

Bautista Smith, J., November 2012. "Strategic Planning and Systems Thinking – Business Sector's Perspective "Using Lean Methodology" ASQ/Education Division, KY – Workshop material.

Bautista Smith, J., October 2012. "Auditing Beyond Compliance," ASQ 21st Audit Conference, GA –Presentation material.

Bautista Smith, J., July 2010. "Rapid Response – The Right Way to Address Customer Complaints," *ASQ/Quality Progress Magazine.*

Bautista Smith, J., August 2012. "The Big Picture – Do not be misled by productivity measures," *ASQ/Quality Progress Magazine.*

Bautista Smith, J., April 2012. "A Case of Mistaken Capability," Article published by iSixSigma.com http://www.isixsigma.com/implementation/case-studies/a-case-of-mistaken-capability/

Bautista Smith, J., 2010 and 2011."Lean Auditing, ASQ 19th and 20th Audit Division conference (2010-Fl), (2011 (NV) - Tutorial workshop.

Bautista Smith, J., March 2010. "Lean Express," ASQ Lean and Six Sigma Conference – AZ.

Coleman, Lance B., Sr. September 2015. "Amazing Audits,"*ASQ/Quality Progress Magazine.*

Customs–Trade Partnership Against Terrorism (C-TPAT) Manual. 2010. U.S. Customs Border Patrol.

International Automotive Task Force and the Technical Committee of ISO. ISO/TS 16949:2009. Quality management systems – Particular requirements for the application of ISO 9001:2008 for automotive production and relevant service part organizations.

ISO 9001:2015 Auditor Transition Training – AQS Management Systems.

Juran, J.M. and A. B. Godfrey. 1999. *Juran's Quality Handbook, 5th Edition,* New York, McGraw Hill.

Kubiak, T.M. and Donald Benbow, 2009. *The Certified Six Sigma Black Belt Handbook,* 2nd Edition, ASQ Quality Press.

Microsoft Products: SmartArt Graphic feature of Microsoft Office Word 2007, Microsoft Visio 2010.

Pyzdek, T., 2003. *The Six Sigma Handbook: Complete Guide for Green Belts, Black Belts and Managers,* New York, McGraw Hill.

Reference for definition of *buoyancy*: http://en.wikipedia.org/wiki/Buoyancy.

Reference for definition of *8-D*: http://asq.org/learn-about-quality/eight-disciplines-8d/

Reference for fishbone diagram: Simon, Kerri http://www.isixsigma.com/tools-templates/cause-effect/cause-and-effect-aka-fishbone-diagram/ http://en.wikipedia.org/wiki/Ishikawa_diagram

Reference for definition of *laminate*: (http://en.wikipedia.org/wiki/Laminate

Reference for definition of *Sequoia tree:* http://en.wikipedia.org/wiki/List_of_largest_giant_sequoias.

Reference for definition of *underlayment:* http://www.ehow.com/info_12161560_purpose-underlayment-beneath-laminate-flooring.html

Sawyer, Ralph D., 1994. *The Art of War (History and Warfare)*, Westview Press.

Society of Automotive Engineers – Aerospace Requirements. 2009 the European Association of Aerospace Industries. SAE T9100 Revision C: AS 9100C Quality Managements.

TL 9000, QMS Requirement, Quest Forum.

U. S. Defense Logistics Agency. 1995. MIL-PRF-31032 Standard for Printed Circuit Board/ Printed Wiring Board, Department of Defense.

Two and A-Half Men TV show, reference to 'if life gives you lemons, make a lemonade!'

Index

Page numbers in *italics* refer to figures or tables.

M

N

O

P-Q

T-U

V

W-Z

The Knowledge Center
www.asq.org/knowledge-center

Learn about quality. Apply it. Share it.

ASQ's online Knowledge Center is the place to:

- Stay on top of the latest in quality with Editor's Picks and Hot Topics.
- Search ASQ's collection of articles, books, tools, training, and more.
- Connect with ASQ staff for personalized help hunting down the knowledge you need, the networking opportunities that will keep your career and organization moving forward, and the publishing opportunities that are the best fit for you.

Use the Knowledge Center Search to quickly sort through hundreds of books, articles, and other software-related publications.

www.asq.org/knowledge-center

TRAINING CERTIFICATION CONFERENCES MEMBERSHIP **PUBLICATIONS**

ASQ
The Global Voice of Quality™

Ask a Librarian

Did you know?

- The ASQ Quality Information Center contains a wealth of knowledge and information available to ASQ members and non-members
- A librarian is available to answer research requests using ASQ's ever-expanding library of relevant, credible quality resources, including journals, conference proceedings, case studies and Quality Press publications
- ASQ members receive free internal information searches and reduced rates for article purchases
- You can also contact the Quality Information Center to request permission to reuse or reprint ASQ copyrighted material, including journal articles and book excerpts
- For more information or to submit a question, visit **http://asq.org/knowledge-center/ask-a-librarian-index**

Visit www.asq.org/qic for more information.

TRAINING CERTIFICATION CONFERENCES MEMBERSHIP **PUBLICATIONS**

ASQ®
The Global Voice of Quality™

Belong to the Quality Community!

Established in 1946, ASQ is a global community of quality experts in all fields and industries. ASQ is dedicated to the promotion and advancement of quality tools, principles, and practices in the workplace and in the community.

The Society also serves as an advocate for quality. Its members have informed and advised the U.S. Congress, government agencies, state legislatures, and other groups and individuals worldwide on quality-related topics.

Vision

By making quality a global priority, an organizational imperative, and a personal ethic, ASQ becomes the community of choice for everyone who seeks quality technology, concepts, or tools to improve themselves and their world.

ASQ is...

- More than 90,000 individuals and 700 companies in more than 100 countries
- The world's largest organization dedicated to promoting quality
- A community of professionals striving to bring quality to their work and their lives
- The administrator of the Malcolm Baldrige National Quality Award
- A supporter of quality in all sectors including manufacturing, service, healthcare, government, and education
- YOU

Visit www.asq.org for more information.

TRAINING CERTIFICATION CONFERENCES MEMBERSHIP **PUBLICATIONS**

ASQ®
The Global Voice of Quality™

ASQ Membership

Research shows that people who join associations experience increased job satisfaction, earn more, and are generally happier*. ASQ membership can help you achieve this while providing the tools you need to be successful in your industry and to distinguish yourself from your competition. So why wouldn't you want to be a part of ASQ?

Networking

Have the opportunity to meet, communicate, and collaborate with your peers within the quality community through conferences and local ASQ section meetings, ASQ forums or divisions, ASQ Communities of Quality discussion boards, and more.

Professional Development

Access a wide variety of professional development tools such as books, training, and certifications at a discounted price. Also, ASQ certifications and the ASQ Career Center help enhance your quality knowledge and take your career to the next level.

Solutions

Find answers to all your quality problems, big and small, with ASQ's Knowledge Center, mentoring program, various e-newsletters, *Quality Progress* magazine, and industry-specific products.

Access to Information

Learn classic and current quality principles and theories in ASQ's Quality Information Center (QIC), *ASQ Weekly* e-newsletter, and product offerings.

Advocacy Programs

ASQ helps create a better community, government, and world through initiatives that include social responsibility, Washington advocacy, and Community Good Works.

Visit www.asq.org/membership for more information on ASQ membership.

*2008, The William E. Smith Institute for Association Research

TRAINING CERTIFICATION CONFERENCES **MEMBERSHIP** **PUBLICATIONS**

ASQ®
The Global Voice of Quality™